As I open this book,
I open myself
to God's presence
in my life.

God's Invitation

God calls me
to be aware of him
in all the people I know,
the places I go,
and the things I do each day.

My Response

When I quiet myself to allow
God's grace to help me,
I see with truth,
hear with forgiveness,
and act with kindness
as God's love works through me.

Thank you God,
for your presence
in my life.

FindingGod

Our response to God's gifts
2

Parish Edition

Barbara F. Campbell, M.Div., D.Min.

James P. Campbell, M.A., D.Min.

LOYOLAPRESS.

CHICAGO

Nihil Obstat Reverend John G. Lodge, S.S.L., S.T.D. Censor Deputatus August 20, 2003	***Imprimatur*** Most Reverend Edwin M. Conway, D.D. Vicar General Archdiocese of Chicago August 22, 2003	**The Ad Hoc Committee to Oversee the Use of the Catechism, United States Conference of Catholic Bishops, has found this catechetical text, copyright 2005, to be in conformity with the *Catechism of the Catholic Church*.**
The *Nihil Obstat* and *Imprimatur* are official declarations that a book is free of doctrinal and moral error. No implication is contained therein that those who have granted the *Nihil Obstat* and *Imprimatur* agree with the content, opinions, or statements expressed. Nor do they assume any legal responsibility associated with publication.		

Finding God: Our Response to God's Gifts is an expression of the work of Loyola Press, an apostolate of the Chicago Province of the Society of Jesus.

Senior Consultants

Jane Regan, Ph.D.
Richard Hauser, S.J., Ph.D., S.T.L.
Robert Fabing, S.J., D.Min.

Advisors

Most Reverend Gordon D. Bennett, S.J., D.D.
George A. Aschenbrenner, S.J., S.T.L.
Paul H. Colloton, O.P., Ph.D.
Eugene LaVerdiere, S.S.S., Ph.D., S.T.L.

Peg Bowman, M.A.
Gerald Darring, M.A.
Brian DuSell, D.M.A.
Teresa DuSell, M.M.
Bryan T. Froehle, Ph.D.

Thomas J. McGrath
Joanne Paprocki, M.A.
Daniel L. Snyder, M.Div., Ph.D.
Christopher R. Weickert
Elaine M. Weickert

Catechetical Staff

Daniel W. Gast, M.A.
Jeanette L. Graham, M.A.
Marlene Halpin, O.P., Ph.D.
Thomas McLaughlin, M.A.
Joseph Paprocki, M.A.

Grateful acknowledgment is given to authors, publishers, photographers, museums, and agents for permission to reprint the following copyrighted material; music credits where appropriate can be found at the bottom of each individual song. Every effort has been made to determine copyright owners. In the case of any omissions, the publisher will be pleased to make suitable acknowledgments in future editions. Continued on page 319.

Cover Design: Think Design Group
Cover Illustration: Christina Balit
Interior Design: Three Communication Design

LOYOLAPRESS.
3441 N. ASHLAND AVENUE
CHICAGO, ILLINOIS 60657
(800) 621-1008
www.LoyolaPress.org
www.FindingGod.org

06 07 08 09 10 11 12 13 Banta 10 9 8 7 6 5 4 3 2

Table of Contents

God Loves Us

Saint Isidore the Farmer

Saint Isidore the Farmer cared for the earth, the plants, and the animals. Although he was poor, Saint Isidore shared what he could with others.

Saint Isidore the Farmer

Saint Isidore and his wife, Saint Maria de la Cabeza, lived on a rich man's farm. Isidore worked for this man his whole life. He took care of the man's land with love. While Isidore worked, he prayed.

Isidore is the patron saint of farmers, farm animals, and farming communities. He is also the patron saint of picnics!

In many places farm animals and crops are blessed on Saint Isidore's Day.

God Creates Us

God is the Creator. He made
heaven and earth. He created
them to show how much he loves us.

God loves everything he makes.
What are some things that God has made?

 Prayer

*God, help me know that you have made all things so
I can see how good and wonderful you are.*

God Made Heaven and Earth

At first there was no earth. There was no warm sun during the day. There was no glowing moon at night. No bright stars were shining in the sky. There was only God—the Father, the Son, and the Holy Spirit.

Then God made the world. He made the sky, the sun, and the moon. He made the sea. God filled it with different kinds of fish. He made the land. He filled it with many kinds of animals.

Then God said, "Let us make someone special."
So God made a man and a woman. He blessed
them and told them to have children. He told
them to take good care of the earth.

God looked at everything he had made.
God was pleased with all he had done.

adapted from Genesis 1:1-31

What Did God Make?

Fill in the blanks to name things God has made.
These things are shown in the picture.

bi__d   __ree   s__y   c__oud   __u__

God's Blessing

Rosa asked her grandmother, "Abuela, why did God make us?"

"Because God is full of love," said Abuela. "He wanted someone to give his love to. He made the world and all things in it. The sun warms the day. Rain makes things grow."

"Yes," said Juanita, Rosa's sister. "There are fruits and plants to eat. There are many wonderful animals to see!"

"People are also part of God's **creation**," said Abuela. "God wants all people to love and care for one another."

Our Loving God

We have been created by a loving God. God is Father, Son, and Holy Spirit. This is called the Trinity. God loves us and cares for us. That is why he stays close to us and in our hearts.

Think of the beautiful story of creation. Picture the good things in the world. Remember that God has loved us from the beginning of the world. We can be **holy** because he loves us.

Reading God's Word

Everything that God made is good. We are thankful for all that God has given us.

adapted from 1 Timothy 4:4

Prayer

God made many things. We praise him with the Glory Be to the Father.

As you pray the Glory Be to the Father, think about how much God loves you and cares for you.

Glory be to the Father, and to the Son, and to the Holy Spirit. As it was in the beginning, is now, and ever shall be, world without end. Amen.

Think about the things we praise God for. Thank God for creating you. Thank him for loving you.

Faith Summary

Because he loves us, God made many things. All of them are good. God wants us to take good care of the world.

Words I Learned

creation   **holy**

Ways of Being Like Jesus

Jesus loves all of us and everything that God made. You are like Jesus when you love all of God's creation.

With My Family

Have a picnic with your family so you can enjoy God's world. Talk about God's creation.

Prayer

Thank you, God, for all you have made. Help me love you by taking care of your creation.

My Response

Draw a picture showing what you will do to take good care of the world this week.

Focus on Faith

God Says That the World Is Good

Children love surprises. They soak up new experiences every day and ask many *why* questions about the way things work. It may not always benefit your child to hear these questions—such as "Why is the sky blue?"—answered only with scientific explanations. Instead, a story about how the blue color of the sky reminds us to honor Jesus' mother, Mary, might sound just right to your child. The first chapter of Genesis is filled with this kind of wonder. God is the great craftsman who created the sun, moon, and stars and said that they are very good. Perhaps even more amazingly, God keeps everything going day after day, and we awake each morning delighted to see that he has done it again. Children are God's happy surprises, and they remind us not to take things for granted.

Dinnertime Conversation Starter

Share your memories of a time when your family discovered something wonderful or beautiful about the world.

Spirituality in Action

Take your child to the zoo or a lush park. Encourage your child to use all of his or her senses to notice the surroundings. Ask your child to make observations about the animals or plants. Then share with one another an appreciation of these wonders that God has made.

Hints for at Home

Work with your child to create a collage representing the natural wonders that God has created. Use magazine clippings, poster board, and other materials to create the collage. Hang it in a special place in your home.

Focus on Prayer

Your child is learning to pray the Doxology, or Glory Be to the Father. Pray the prayer together often as a family to facilitate memorization. Begin the Glory Be to the Father with the Sign of the Cross.

God Gives Us Jesus

Did you ever receive a special gift from a friend or family member? How happy did it make you?

Prayer

Dear God, help me always remember the gifts you have given me.

The Story of Joseph

Before Joseph and Mary were married, an angel appeared to Joseph in a dream. The angel told Joseph that the baby which Mary was going to have would be from the Holy Spirit.

Joseph did not understand. Then the angel said, "Joseph, son of David, do not be afraid to take Mary as your wife."

adapted from Matthew 1:18-20

 Reading God's Word

I will be with you always, until the end of the world!

adapted from Matthew 28:20

The angel told Joseph to name the child Jesus. The name *Jesus* means "God saves" or "God saves us." Because Jesus will save us from our sins, he is our **Savior.**

After Joseph woke up from his dream, he took Mary as his wife.

adapted from Matthew 1:21-24

Word Puzzle

Unscramble these letters to spell names from the Bible story you have just read.

Jsoeph __ __ __ __ __ __

suJes __ __ __ __ __

ryMa __ __ __ __

Another Name

Jesus would also be called **Emmanuel**. *Emmanuel* means "God with us."

Names for Jesus

Jesus is known by many names. Each of them has a special meaning. Choose a word from the box to complete each meaning. The first one is done for you.

~~blessed~~	God	saves	with

NAME and MEANING

Christ = <u>blessed</u> by God

Emmanuel = God _____ us

Jesus = _____ saves

Savior = one who _____ us

A Precious Gift

You know that God has given us many things. The most precious gift he has given us is his Son, Jesus. God gave Jesus to the whole world.

As God's Son who became man, Jesus wants to help us live good lives. Because of Jesus, we have been saved from our sins. He can help us live with God in heaven one day.

Jesus is with us in the **Blessed Sacrament.** We **genuflect** to honor the Blessed Sacrament inside the **tabernacle.**

Link to Liturgy

When the Mass begins, the priest says, "The Lord be with you." We respond by saying, "And also with you."

Prayer

Imagine that you are with Joseph and Mary in the stable where Jesus was born.

You are holding Jesus carefully and gently close to your heart. You know that you can tell him whatever you would like. What do you whisper to him? Do you sing to him?

Jesus loves you. You listen with your heart to what he wants you to know. You are happy together.

Faith Summary

Because of God's great love for us, he sent his Son to become man. Jesus is God's greatest gift to the world. Jesus is our Savior.

Words I Learned

Blessed Sacrament   **Emmanuel**
genuflect   **Savior**   **tabernacle**

Ways of Being Like Jesus

We are blessed to be part of the human family. You are like Jesus when you love and respect people.

With My Family

Make a gift or card for someone in your family. On it write "I love you."

Living My Faith

Prayer

Thank you, God, for sending us Jesus. Please show me how to be more like him.

My Response

Write a sentence about what you will do to help others.

Saint Joseph Shadow of the Father,
William Hart McNichols

Focus on Faith

God Trusts Joseph With Jesus

The Gospel of Matthew tells us that Joseph was a man one could trust. He was open to hearing God's revelation that Jesus would be the one who saves us. God trusted Joseph to care for Jesus and Mary. Joseph may have helped Jesus take his first steps. We can imagine Joseph walking through the village with Jesus' hand firmly in his. Joseph taught Jesus about the history of their people and what it means to be faithful to God. As parents, we have been entrusted with children who are precious to God. We are their anchors in a hectic world, and our firm and loving hold on their hands as we walk together communicates to them the loving presence of the God who saves.

Spirituality in Action

With your child prepare a package of nonperishable foods to deliver to a local food pantry. Explain to your child the importance of helping those who are less fortunate.

Dinnertime Conversation Starter

Discuss what it must have been like for Jesus to learn from Joseph how to be a carpenter. What do you think Joseph would have taught him first? Discuss things that you learn from each family member.

Hints for at Home

Work with your family to create an I Caught You Being Like Jesus bulletin board. Cut out hearts of colored paper and keep them in a special place, such as a basket with a marker tied to it. When one member of the family "catches" another being kind, loving, generous, or thoughtful, encourage him or her to write the name of the "caught" family member, along with a brief explanation of the Jesus-like act, on a heart. Post the hearts on a bulletin board.

Focus on Prayer

The story of Joseph reminds us of the immense love that the Holy Family had for God and for one another. As God directed him through an angel, Joseph took Mary as his wife and helped to bring up Jesus with great care. Through Joseph we learn the importance of family and of doing God's will. Spend a few moments together in quiet reflection, examining Joseph's dedication to God and to his family.

God Is Our Father

Think about your family, your home, and the food you eat. In what ways has God taken care of you?

 Prayer

Dear Jesus, help me know and love God our Father as you did.

Trust in God

Jesus wants us to know that God our Father is close to us. Jesus helps us learn to trust in God.

Jesus said, "Do not worry about your life. Do not worry about what you will eat or drink or what you will wear. Worrying will not add one minute to your life.

"See the birds that fly and the flowers that grow. The birds in the sky do not work. Yet God gives them the food they need to live.

"Be like the flowers that grow wild. They do not work. But God helps them grow strong. God provides for all of them. And he will provide for you."

adapted from Matthew 6:25-34

Color God's Creatures

Color the birds and flowers in the picture.

Reading God's Word

Trust in the power of God. Place all your cares in his hands because he cares for you.

adapted from 1 Peter 5:6-7

God Cares for Us

Jesus called God Father just as some children call their fathers Dad. Jesus reminds us that God is our Father too. God loves us and wants us to be happy. He wants all the best for us.

God gives birds the food they need to live. The flowers grow strong and lovely with God's care.

 Link to Liturgy

During Mass, we stand to pray the Lord's Prayer. We pray this prayer together.

When we **petition** God in prayer, we ask him for what we need. We pray to God to help us.

It is also good to **praise** God in our prayers. We tell him how wonderful he is.

God is our Creator and Father. We are his children. He cares for all people of the world because he is everyone's Father.

Jesus was a good Son. He listened to all that his Father said. Jesus had trust in God. He reminds us to trust God too.

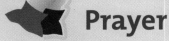

Prayer

In prayer we talk to and listen to God. We praise God, our loving Father, and we ask him for what we need. Jesus gave us the words to the Lord's Prayer, or the Our Father. You can praise God with this prayer and bring your needs to him.

As you pray, keep in mind how much God our Father loves us.

Lord's Prayer

*Our Father,
who art in heaven,
hallowed be thy name;
thy kingdom come;
thy will be done on earth
    as it is in heaven.
Give us this day our daily bread;
and forgive us our trespasses
as we forgive those
    who trespass against us;
and lead us not into temptation,
but deliver us from evil.
       Amen.*

Faith Summary

Jesus helps us learn that God is our loving Father and is close to us. Jesus tells us to trust in God and place our cares in God's hands.

Words I Learned

petition   praise

Ways of Being Like Jesus

Jesus was a good son to God the Father. He obeyed his Father. You are like Jesus when you listen to your parents.

With My Family

Help care for the birds of the sky. Place a bird feeder in your yard.

Living My Faith

Prayer

Thank you, Jesus, for teaching me to trust in God and to place my cares in his hands.

My Response

Draw a picture or write a sentence to describe a care you would like to place in God's hands.

RAISING FAITH-FILLED KIDS

a parent page

Focus on Faith

Teach Me to Pray

We are all beginners in prayer. No matter how many years we have been praying, we feel like rookies before God. We wonder what to say, what to do, what to say next, and whether we are being heard at all. This is what the disciples must have felt when they approached Jesus and asked him to teach them to pray. Jesus' response was to teach the Lord's Prayer. He would teach us the same thing today. Jesus wants us to know that no one loves us more than God does. God is always ready to listen, to forgive, and to help us forgive others. However we pray or teach our children to pray, prayer means to be open to love and share that love with others.

Dinnertime Conversation Starter

Talk together about the things each of you would like to ask God for. Ask each family member to pray to God for one thing.

Hints for at Home

Help God take care of the birds of the sky. With your child create birdie treats. You will need peanut butter, birdseed, nylon netting, and twine. Combine a cup of peanut butter with a cup and a half of birdseed to form a thick, dry mixture. Divide the mixture into four pieces and roll each into a ball. Place each ball into a piece of nylon netting and tie the opening with a long piece of twine. Tie the opposite end of the twine to a tree branch and watch God's creatures enjoy your creation!

Focus on Prayer

Your child is learning to pray the Lord's Prayer, or the Our Father. Pray the prayer together often as a family to build memorization. At Mass help your child watch for the special gestures the priest uses during the Our Father. The words to the Lord's Prayer are found at www.FindingGod.org.

Spirituality in Action

As children of God, we are part of one human family. Take your child to visit a nursing home or a homebound member of your community. Explain to your child that showing concern and kindness for others is a way to remain connected to our larger human family.

God's Life for Us

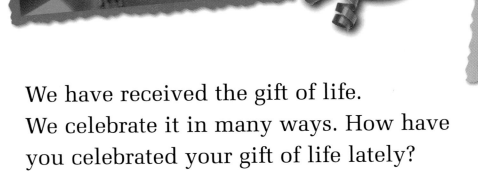

We have received the gift of life.
We celebrate it in many ways. How have
you celebrated your gift of life lately?

Prayer

*Dear God, bring me closer to your Holy Spirit so that
I can remember he is always with me.*

Simeon of Jerusalem

There was a man named Simeon who lived in Jerusalem.

Simeon loved God. He listened to the Holy Spirit. The Spirit promised that Simeon would not die until he had seen the **Messiah.**

One day Simeon was in the **Temple.** Mary and Joseph came with the baby Jesus. Simeon saw them enter the Temple. Simeon saw that Mary was carrying Jesus.

Guided by the grace of the Holy Spirit, Simeon knew that Jesus was the Savior.

Simeon took Jesus into his arms. He praised God and said, "Now, Master, you may let your servant go in peace. My eyes have seen the Savior. He is the one you have promised to all people."

adapted from Luke 2:25-32

Simeon's Story

Draw a line to match important words from the story of Simeon.

1. Simeon loved God and listened to the ●

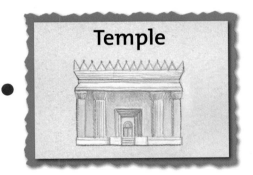

Temple

2. God's promise to all people is ●

Holy Spirit

3. Simeon was in the ●

Jesus

The Holy Spirit

The Holy Spirit is here to guide us, as he guided Simeon. The Spirit helps us know that God is always with us.

 **Reading God's Word**

You will be my light to the ends of the earth so that all people may be saved.

adapted from Isaiah 49:6

The Holy Spirit also gives us **faith** in God. By listening to the Spirit, we learn to care for ourselves and others, as God wants us to.

❓ Did You Know?

The name *Simeon* means "God has heard."

Prayer

The Holy Spirit is in your heart, waiting to guide you. Ask the Holy Spirit for help by praying this prayer.

Come, Holy Spirit, fill the hearts of your faithful.
And kindle in them the fire of your love.
Send forth your Spirit and they shall be created.
And you will renew the face of the earth.

Ask the Holy Spirit to fill your heart with love. Thank him for being your guide.

Faith Summary

The Holy Spirit is present in our lives. When we listen to the Spirit, we recognize God in ordinary things around us.

Words I Learned

faith   Messiah   Temple

Ways of Being Like Jesus

Jesus knew that God is all around us in many ordinary things. You are like Jesus when you see God in the world around you.

With My Family

Show your care for your family. Rake leaves or do other yard work.

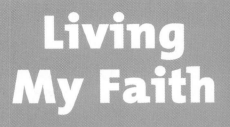

Living My Faith

Prayer

Holy Spirit, thank you for being my guide. Help me to always listen to you and to do what you want me to do.

My Response

Draw a picture to show how you can take care of someone this week.

a parent page

Focus on Faith

Seeing People for Who They Are

We all live with stereotypes. It is easy to make assumptions and to label people according to their looks, clothes, or ethnic origins. In this session your child read about Joseph and Mary's coming with the baby Jesus to the Temple. Their humble offering of two turtledoves immediately labeled them as poor and unimportant, and this is how most people saw them. Simeon, inspired by the Holy Spirit, saw beneath the surface to recognize the promised Messiah in Jesus. The Holy Spirit also calls us to see everyone through the eyes of faith and to discover how each person is sacred and loved by God. When you look at your child today, whom do you see? How can you nurture the sacred person within your child?

Dinnertime Conversation Starter

Discuss a movie or television show you have all seen in which a character starts out looking like a villain but is revealed as a hero at the end. Explore together what this can tell us about looking beyond first impressions.

The Presentation of Christ in the Temple, Vittore Carpaccio

Focus on Prayer

Your child is learning the Prayer to the Holy Spirit. In this prayer we ask the Spirit to remain

with us through everything we do, say, and think. The prayer reminds us to call on the Spirit for guidance when we are experiencing struggles or difficulties in our lives. Pray the prayer together and invite your child to discuss what it means to him or her. The words to the Prayer to the Holy Spirit are found at www.FindingGod.org.

Hints for at Home

Create and display a simple family tree. Include grandparents, aunts and uncles, and cousins. Talk about how your family members reflect God's presence in your lives. You might add items that reflect God's presence in the ordinary. For example, you might include pine cones, seashells, twigs, and leaves in the display. You might add pictures of your immediate and extended families as well as family pets. Over time, continue to add to your display.

Our Catholic Heritage

Your child has read the story of Simeon in the Temple (Luke 2:25–32). The message of the story is that Simeon, guided by faith, was able to recognize the presence of God in the ordinary. Although he saw a poor, helpless baby, Simeon, inspired by the Holy Spirit, recognized Jesus as the Messiah. Read the story with your child. Spend a few moments together thinking about the ways we might recognize God in the people we see every day.

Review

God is our Creator and Father.
He created heaven and earth because
of his great love for us. He gave us his
only Son, Jesus Christ, as our Savior.
How can we thank God for all he
has given us?

Prayer

*God, our Father, I thank you for your gifts. Help me love
you so much that I think of you often.*

Faith Summary

God made many good things because he loves
us. He sent us his Son, Jesus. Jesus saves us
from our sins.

Jesus helps us learn more about God. Jesus wants
us to know that God is close to us. God is in our
hearts. God loves us.

The Holy Spirit is always with us. Through
the Holy Spirit, we can learn to care for others.

Review Search

Circle the important names and words in the puzzle. These words are found below.

FAITH	GOD	HOLY	JESUS
JOSEPH	MARY	MESSIAH	PRAISE

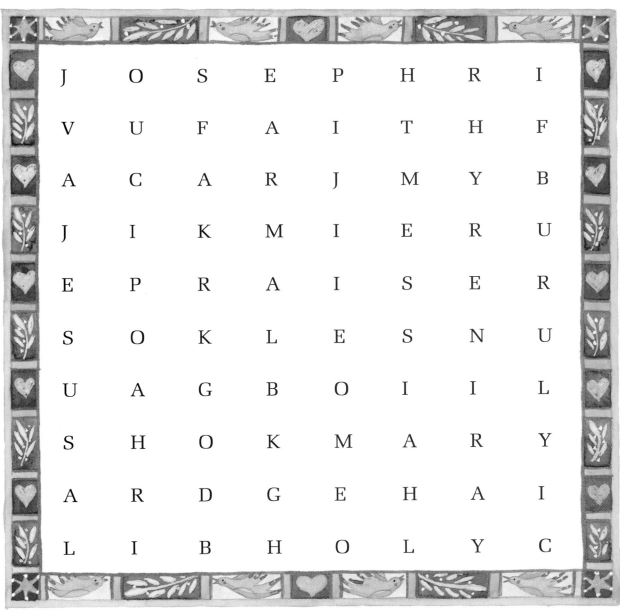

J	O	S	E	P	H	R	I
V	U	F	A	I	T	H	F
A	C	A	R	J	M	Y	B
J	I	K	M	I	E	R	U
E	P	R	A	I	S	E	R
S	O	K	L	E	S	N	U
U	A	G	B	O	I	I	L
S	H	O	K	M	A	R	Y
A	R	D	G	E	H	A	I
L	I	B	H	O	L	Y	C

Trinity Knots

Celtic knots were used in art by monks in Ireland long ago. Each knot had a special meaning. The Trinity Knot represented the Holy Trinity.

This Trinity Knot will remind you that God—the Father, the Son, and the Holy Spirit—cares for you. Color the picture and cut it out. Hang it in a special place.

Prayer Service

Leader: *Praise be to God, who fills our lives with joy.*

All: *Amen.*

Leader: *Water was used when we were baptized. It reminds us that God created everything.*

All: *Amen.*

Leader: *A reading from the Book of Genesis.*

Then God said, "Let the water under the sky be gathered into a single basin, so that the dry land may appear." [Genesis 1:9]

The Word of the Lord.

All: *Thanks be to God.*

Leader: *Together let us pray the Lord's Prayer.*

Living My Faith

Ways of Being Like Jesus

Jesus knew the power of gentle words and actions. You are like Jesus when you speak to others with respect and show them kindness.

With My Family

Practice acting like Jesus with your family. Say a kind thing about each member of your family. Watch him or her smile!

Prayer

Dear God, thank you for all you have given me. Help me share your love with others.

My Response

What would you like to thank God for? Draw a picture and write a sentence to go with it.

Jesus Loves Us

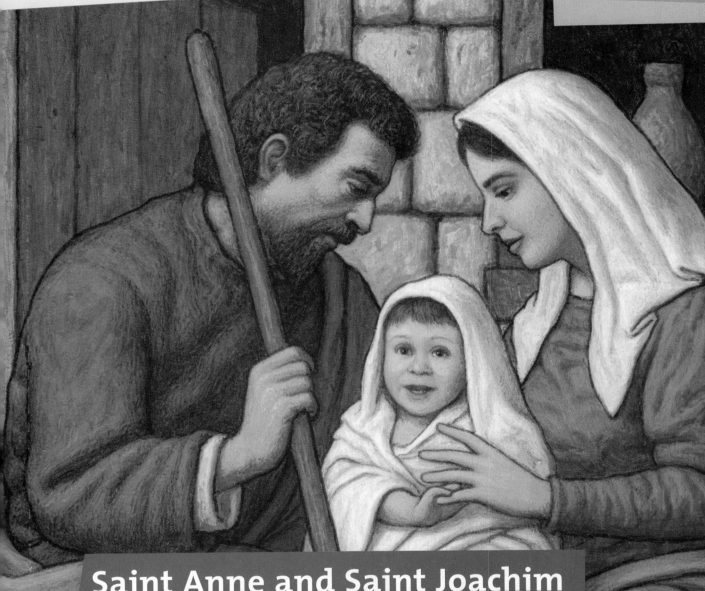

Saint Anne and Saint Joachim

Anne and Joachim were Mary's parents. They raised Mary to have a strong faith and a great love for God.

Saint Anne and Saint Joachim

Mary was devoted to God. She learned this devotion from her own parents, Anne and Joachim.

Mary listened to God and became the mother of Jesus. She was open to God because of her faith and the faith of her parents.

Saint Anne is the patron saint of mothers. She is also the patron saint of women who are expecting babies. Saint Joachim is the patron saint of fathers.

Jesus Is Faithful

What are some ways you have obeyed your parents? What are some chores you have helped with?

 Prayer

Jesus, Son of God, give me the grace to love God and to be faithful to him.

Jesus With the Teachers

When Jesus was 12 years old, he went with his parents to Jerusalem. They were celebrating a festival. When the festival was over, Mary and Joseph headed for home with their friends.

Mary and Joseph thought Jesus was traveling with them. They looked for him, but they could not find him. They became very worried.

Mary and Joseph returned to Jerusalem to look for Jesus. After three days they found him in the Temple.

adapted from Luke 2:41-46

❓ Did You Know?

The Temple was the most important place of worship for the Jewish people.

Jesus was sitting with the teachers, listening to them and asking questions. When his parents saw him, they were amazed.

Mary asked, "Son, why did you do this to us? We were very worried about you."

Jesus said, "I must do what my Father wants me to do." His parents did not completely understand.

Jesus returned home with Mary and Joseph. Mary remembered what happened. Jesus grew older and wiser.

adapted from Luke 2:47-52

Jesus the Good Son

Jesus realized that he should obey his parents and not cause them to worry. That is why he went home with them and always did what they asked.

Like Jesus, you should listen to and obey your parents. Ask Jesus to help you obey them.

Finding Jesus

Use the words in the box to tell about when Mary and Joseph found Jesus.

Mary	Temple	three

1. the number of days that Jesus was missing

   —— —— —— —— ——

2. the person who looked for Jesus

   —— —— —— ——

3. where Jesus was found

   —— —— —— —— —— ——

God's Special Rules

Jesus, Mary, and Joseph were followers of the Jewish faith. They accepted the **Ten Commandments** and always obeyed them. As Catholics, we also are to follow the Ten Commandments. We follow Jesus when we obey the Commandments. Our **conscience** guides us to do what the Commandments tell us.

 **Reading God's Word**

Honor your mother and father so that you may live a long life.

adapted from Exodus 20:12

Prayer

Jesus was at home in the Temple. This was the special place where he could worship God the Father.

You have a special place where you can go to worship God the Father too. The next time you go to church, take time to be quiet before or after Mass. Make this your special time and place to be with God your Father. Imagine how happy he is to be with you!

Picture yourself in church. Thank God that you are his child. Be still with your heavenly Father.

Faith Summary

Jesus was faithful to the Ten Commandments. They help us love God and others.

Words I Learned

conscience   Ten Commandments

Ways of Being Like Jesus

Jesus honored his parents, obeyed them, and helped them. You are like Jesus when you follow his example.

With My Family

Show your love for your family. Every time someone does something nice for you, do something nice for another person.

 Prayer

Thank you, God, for giving us your Commandments. Help me to obey you as Jesus did.

My Response

Write a sentence to show what you can do to obey your parents.

Focus on Faith

Jesus' Obedience and Ours

Jesus was a faithful Jewish boy who loved and obeyed his parents. We like to emphasize this when we talk to our children. We tell them that they should be obedient to their parents, just as Jesus was obedient to his. The root word for *obedience* means "to hear or to listen." As parents, we need to listen carefully to our children in order to recognize their concerns and respond to them. Becoming a good listener is one obligation we have if we are to raise our children in the ways that Jesus wants. As Christian parents, we have authority over our children. We are called to exercise this authority by nurturing our children's growth in the Christian life.

Dinnertime Conversation Starter

Explain to your children that you are always ready to listen, whether they have good or bad news. Tell them that their honesty is more important than any mistake they might make. Be sure not to criticize them when they are honest. Instead, discuss what they should do in the future to act according to Jesus' teaching.

Hints for at Home

Help your child create a Time for Prayer clock. You will need a paper plate, crayons or markers, construction paper, scissors, and a brass fastener. With crayons or markers, decorate the paper plate to look like a clock. Create praying hour and minute hands by tracing your child's hands, fingers together, onto the paper. Cut out the hands and attach them to the center of the clock with the fastener, and hang the clock in a special place. You may wish to designate a special family prayer time, such as before dinner or at bedtime. You may also allow time for prayer when the moment is appropriate, such as when asking for guidance or expressing special thanks.

Our Catholic Heritage

Catholicism has developed into a truly global religion. For example, in recent years Catholicism has shown tremendous growth in Africa. Approximately 390 million people in Africa are Christian; of those, roughly 115 million are Catholic. As recently as the early to mid 1990s, there were fewer than 100 million Catholics in Africa.

Focus on Prayer

The family provides a nurturing environment in which your child can learn to pray. Be a positive role model. Guide your child to understand that speaking and listening to God can be done at any moment.

Jesus Saves Us

What are some good things you have done for your family? What good things has your family done for you?

 Prayer

Jesus, my friend, walk with me as I learn to follow your example of love and goodness.

Jesus Heals

Jesus helped many people who were in need.
He gave sight to those who could not see.
He healed people who could not walk.

At the same time there was a holy man named
John the Baptist. He was teaching people
about the coming of the Messiah.

Some of John's followers told him
about Jesus. So John sent them to
ask Jesus, "Are you the one we
are waiting for, or should we
keep looking?"

adapted from Luke 7:18-21

Did You Know?

Water is the most important symbol of
Baptism.

Jesus said to John's followers, "Go and tell John what you have seen and heard. The blind see again. The sick get well. The deaf hear, and the dead are raised. The poor hear the good news that God loves them."

adapted from Luke 7:22

How Can You Be Like Jesus?

Below are stories about people in need. Write a **J** on the line that shows what you can do to be like Jesus.

1. A person is caught in the rain with no umbrella.

   _____ Share your umbrella.

   _____ Turn your back and walk away.

2. Your father is fixing the front door at home.

   _____ Play video games.

   _____ Get tools for your father.

3. A friend from class does not understand the homework assignment.

   _____ Explain the assignment to your friend.

   _____ Tell everybody that your friend is going to fail.

Jesus Cares for Everybody

Jesus followed God, obeyed Mary and Joseph, and helped people in need. Jesus told people that God loved them. He had a special love for those who were sick. Jesus showed God's love for the sick by healing them.

But some people became angry with Jesus. They put him to death on a cross.

When Jesus died on the cross, everybody thought it was the end of his life. But God raised Jesus from the dead.

Jesus Is Alive

Now Jesus is alive in heaven. He is also with us, helping and caring for us. He wants us to love others as he loves us.

How can you follow Jesus' example of love? How can you care for those around you?

Reading God's Word

The eyes of the blind and the ears of the deaf will be opened.

adapted from Isaiah 35:5

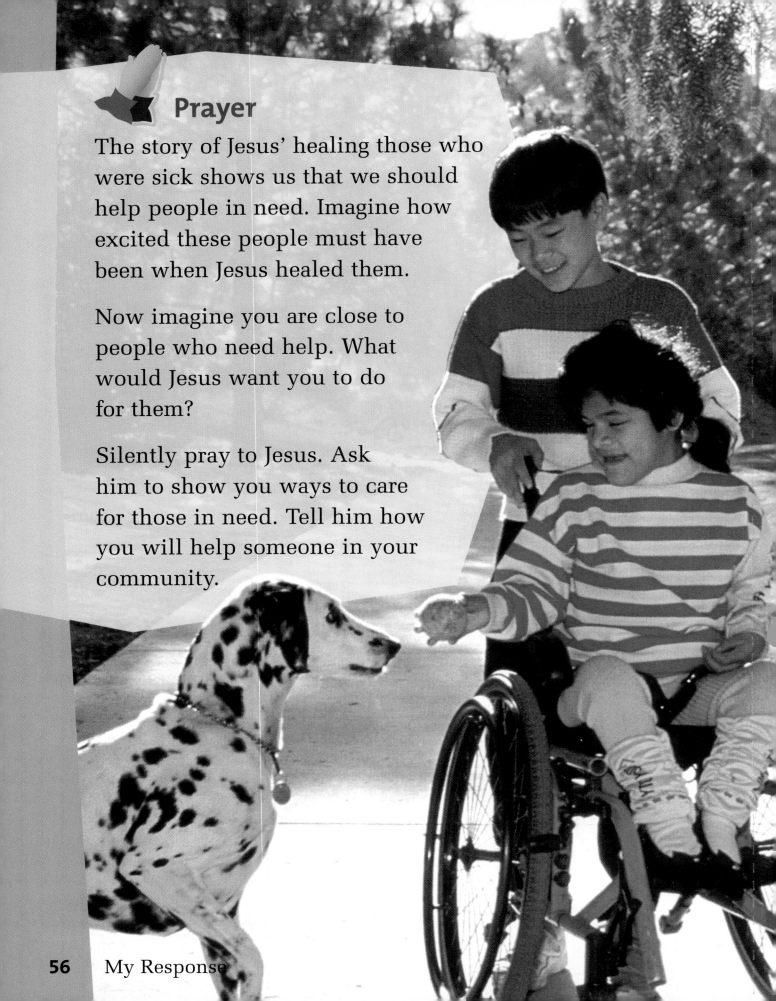

Prayer

The story of Jesus' healing those who were sick shows us that we should help people in need. Imagine how excited these people must have been when Jesus healed them.

Now imagine you are close to people who need help. What would Jesus want you to do for them?

Silently pray to Jesus. Ask him to show you ways to care for those in need. Tell him how you will help someone in your community.

Faith Summary

Jesus is alive in heaven. He helps us to love others.

Ways of Being Like Jesus

Jesus helped those in need. Look around you at others who might need help. Can you help your brother or sister with homework?

With My Family

With your family, spend time visiting a local nursing home.

 Prayer

Thank you, Jesus, for showing me your loving ways, so that I can share your love with others.

My Response

What is one thing you can do to reach out to someone else? Draw a picture.

a parent page

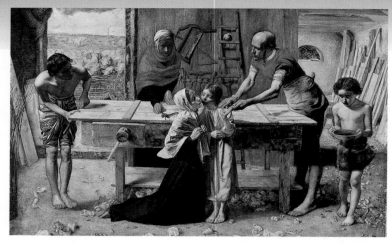

Christ in the House of His Parents, Sir John Everett Millais

Focus on Faith

Jesus' Life and Ours

We do not know very much about Jesus' life on earth. We know about his birth, a little of his infancy, and of one event when he was about 12. Then we learn more about Jesus when he was about 30. Details of Jesus' life are quite scarce. Like any Jewish boy of his time, Jesus learned the traditions of his people. He learned a trade. He obeyed his mother and father. Most of his days, like most of ours, were probably filled with the ordinary things that people do. The simplicity of his life shows us that ordinary days are grace-filled days. In the midst of everyday life, Jesus prepared for his mission. God is also present in our everyday lives. In the loving families that we help God to nurture, ordinary life becomes sacred.

Dinnertime Conversation Starter

Discuss a good deed that someone in your family observed today. Did someone help when an accident happened? Did someone share a snack? Did this deed inspire your family member to do something good?

Spirituality in Action

Create an Every Penny Counts! can for your family to help those in need. Decorate a piece of construction paper, label it *Every Penny Counts!*, and glue it to an empty can. Invite members of your family to place a portion of their weekly allowances or earnings in the can. When the can is full, donate the money you have collected to a charitable group.

Hints for at Home

Jesus said,
    "Do to others whatever you would have them do to you." (Matthew 7:12)

With your family, make a Being Good to Others cross as a reminder to treat people as Jesus teaches. You will need construction paper, scissors, crayons, and glue.
    First, cut a cross out of the construction paper. Then have each family member draw and cut a heart shape from a separate sheet of paper. On his or her heart, each person should write one way to be good to others. Glue the hearts to the cross and discuss how each idea follows what Jesus teaches us about treating other people as we want to be treated.

Focus on Prayer

Your child has been reflecting on the ways in which Jesus led a life of total commitment to God. Spend a few quiet moments of reflection with your child as you think of ways you and your family might share the love of Jesus with one another.

Jesus Calls Us to Love

When have you been invited to a party? Were you happy to be invited?

It's a birthday party!

Please Come!
July 14
1:00 pm

Prayer

Loving Jesus, help me learn to follow you and care for people as you do.

The Parable of the Banquet

Jesus often told a **parable**, or story, to teach an important lesson. He told this parable to show how God wants everyone to be close to him.

A man planned a dinner party and invited many people. When the day of the party came, the man sent his servant to tell the guests, "Come, everything is ready."

One by one, the guests made excuses. The first one said, "Sorry, but I just bought some land. I have to go check it." Another said, "I just bought some animals that I have to take care of." A third one said, "I cannot keep my new wife waiting."

The servant reported this to the master. The master got very angry. He said, "Go out quickly into the town. Bring the poor and the sick, the blind and the lame."

The servant returned and said, "Sir, I followed your orders. There is still room for more guests."

The master said, "Go out to the streets and highways. Have people come and fill my house."

adapted from Luke 14:16-23

Jesus Invites Us

The man in the story invited many guests. Jesus told this parable to teach us that God loves everyone. Everyone is invited to follow God.

Jesus' Invitation

You have received Jesus' invitation to be close to him. What is he inviting you to do? What is your response? Write it on the lines below.

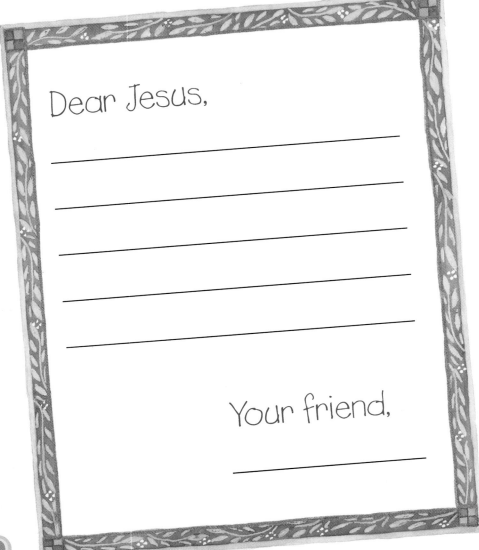

Dear Jesus,

_____

_____

_____

_____

Your friend,

_____

 Meet a Saint

Saint Martin de Porres spent his life helping others in Peru. By caring for others, Martin followed Jesus.

Jesus Chose Peter

Peter was one of the first followers of Jesus. Peter knew that Jesus was the Messiah. Jesus chose Peter to become the leader of the Church.

Peter's role as leader of the Church has been passed on through the years. Today, the **pope** leads the Church as Peter did.

 Reading God's Word

Jesus traveled through Galilee. He taught people, shared God's message, and cured those who were sick.

adapted from Matthew 4:23

Prayer

Jesus tells us how much God loves and cares for us. Think about how we can share his love and his care with everybody we meet.

Think of people in your life who love you. Just as they love you, God too loves you and wants you to be happy. Think of some of the ways God has cared for you.

Now ask God to help you care for others as he cares for you. Tell him one way you will help another person.

Faith Summary

Jesus came to invite everyone to follow God. He chose Peter to lead the Church. We follow God by helping those in need.

Words I Learned

parable   pope

Ways of Being Like Jesus

You are like Jesus when you do a kind deed or say a kind word.

With My Family

Ask your family to invite someone to dinner. Invite a person who does not usually eat with your family.

Prayer

Thank you, Jesus, for helping me to know how much God loves me.

My Response

How can you care for others as God cares for you? Draw a picture.

Focus on Faith

Welcoming the Stranger

What does it mean to serve the Kingdom of God? The following story helps us answer this question. A brother and sister were talking at a family reunion. The brother had drifted away from the Church but liked to argue points of Christian doctrine. The sister was a member of a prayerful religious community that cared for others. The brother tried to engage his sister in an intellectual debate about God and Christianity. She told him that she wasn't interested in debating these issues. She told him that if he wanted to discover what she thought about God, he should spend time with her community and join in her life of service. By extending this invitation, she was asking him to become a participant in serving the Kingdom of God.

Dinnertime Conversation Starter

Discuss with your child whom you might pray for today. How can you help others feel welcome after Mass or at school?

Spirituality in Action

Consider the needs of those in your parish who might require special care, particularly the elderly. Work with your child to create a special Bag of Cheer for an elderly person. Use a brown bag and decorate the outside with drawings or pictures from magazines. Invite your child to print a cheerful message on the bag. Then fill the bag with special gifts of cheer such as tea bags, cookies, holy cards, homemade bookmarks and sample-size toiletry items. Deliver the package with your child.

Hints for at Home

As God's creation, we are all reflections of his love. As we seek to be more like Jesus, we can spread God's love to others. Create a sign that reads "I am reflecting the love of Jesus!" Post the sign over a mirror in your home as a reminder that your family can spread love and kindness each day.

Focus on Prayer

Help your child learn the importance of respecting people with special needs.

Jesus Cares for Us

Think of a time you lost something.
Where did you search for it?
How did you feel when you found it?

 Prayer

Jesus, help me recognize all the ways God cares for me.

The Parable of the Lost Sheep

Jesus said, "Always remember that each person is important to God. An angel in heaven watches over each of them."

Jesus continued, "What do you think about this? A man has a hundred sheep. If one of them gets lost, he will leave the other 99 and search for the one lost sheep."

Jesus went on, "And if he finds that lost sheep, he is happier with it than he is with the other 99 sheep."

"That is also what your heavenly Father wants. He does not want one single person to be lost."

adapted from Matthew 18:10-14

 ## Reading God's Word

I am the good shepherd. A good shepherd lays down his life for the sheep.

John 10:11

Leaders of the Church

Like shepherds, leaders of the Catholic Church care for their people. The pope is the leader of the whole Church.

A **bishop** is another important Church leader. A bishop cares for many parishes. He tends to the needs of Catholics who belong to those parishes. Each bishop carries a shepherd's staff called a **crozier**.

Priests help the bishop with his duties. Priests and **deacons** serve the people in their parishes. They teach about God and lead the people in prayer. Religious sisters and brothers, teachers, and catechists also help people learn about God.

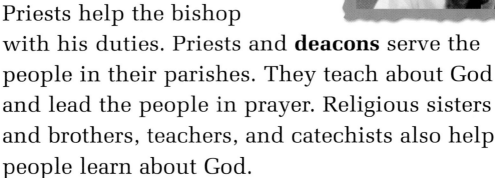

Did You Know?

The crozier that the bishop carries reminds us that he has a duty to care for his people. In this way, the bishop is like the Good Shepherd.

Find the Lost Sheep

A good shepherd cares about every sheep.
Solve the maze to lead this good shepherd
to his lost sheep.

Prayer

The Book of Psalms is a section of the Bible. Psalms are special songs or prayers. Psalm 23 praises God. Let us pray this psalm together.

Lord, you are my shepherd,
    there is nothing that I need.
You make sure I have enough to eat,
    you see that I have good water to drink,
    you give me great strength.
You guide me along the right path,
    so that I may do as you wish.
Even when I am in danger,
    I am not afraid because you are with me,
    your care gives me courage.

[adapted from Psalm 23]

God is the Good Shepherd. He will always take care of you. Thank God for loving you so much.

Faith Summary

Jesus teaches us about God's loving concern for us. The leaders of the Church help us to know and love God.

Words I Learned

bishop　　crozier　　deacon

Ways of Being Like Jesus

You are like Jesus when you include others in your work or play.

With My Family

Plan a special day for someone in your family. Let that person choose the activities.

Prayer

Thank you, God, for being my Good Shepherd and for always staying by my side.

My Response

What can you do to include others in your work or play? Write a sentence.

The Good Shepherd, Elizabeth Lee Hudgins

Focus on Faith

Educators of Our Children

As parents, we are our children's primary teachers in the ways of the faith. This is a huge responsibility, and we have the tendency to think that it requires an extensive knowledge of every aspect of the Catholic Church. Thankfully, the entire burden does not fall on our shoulders. The Church has the support system of parishes, pastors, catechists, and religious education classes. Our role is to focus on the decisions we make every day. Our decisions should exemplify how a Christian should live. Are we honest in our dealings with our children? Do we keep our word with them? Do they see us dealing honestly with others? All decisions we make in daily life shape the religious growth of our children. We cannot help but be their primary teachers in the ways of our faith.

Dinnertime Conversation Starter

Discuss ways in which you as individuals can each be a source of blessing to one another and to others in the world.

Hints for at Home

Make a The Lord Is My Shepherd picture. You'll need felt, markers, scissors, a picture of your child, glue, a paper plate, and a small picture hook. Using the felt, help your child draw and cut out figures to represent a shepherd and a child. Include a crozier, or staff, for the shepherd. Glue the picture of your child's face onto the figure of the child. Draw a face on the shepherd. Glue both figures to the inside of the paper plate. With the marker write the words *The Lord Is My Shepherd* around the outside of the paper plate. Attach a small hook to the back of the plate and hang it.

Our Catholic Heritage

Saint Patrick (380–461) was the son of a Roman nobleman. He was kidnapped by Irish pirates at age 16 and was taken to Ireland. Suffering from cold, hunger, and the loss of his freedom, he worked as a shepherd in Ireland. He eventually escaped and became a priest. He returned to Ireland as a missionary, or shepherd of the people. He established monasteries, convents, and parishes. Saint Patrick is one of the primary reasons that Ireland became a Christian nation.

Focus on Prayer

Your child has read an adapted version of Psalm 23, commonly known as The Lord Is My Shepherd. Read Psalm 23 with your child and discuss the feelings of safety and security that it provides us.

Review

Jesus is the Son of God
and the son of Mary. Jesus
is our friend and Savior.
Through his example of love
and goodness, we can follow
God's way. What can you do
to show your love for Jesus?

 Prayer

*Thank you, Jesus, for watching over me. Help me obey
God and my parents.*

Faith Summary

Jesus obeyed the Ten Commandments. He obeyed his heavenly Father and Mary and Joseph.

Jesus did all he could to help others. We can follow his example and discover the goodness in others.

Jesus told the parable of the lost sheep to show God's concern for us. He gave us our pope, bishops, and priests to care for us.

Jesus calls everyone to follow God. Everyone is welcome.

People Who Served God

Peter served God and others. The sentence in the orange box tells about Peter. In the blue box write the name of another important person you have learned about in this unit. Then write a sentence about this person.

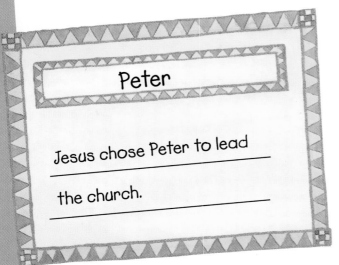

Peter

Jesus chose Peter to lead
the church.

Be Like Jesus

Read each of the sentences below. On the lines write what you could do to be like Jesus.

Your friend has broken her arm.

_____

_____

_____

You see your neighbor shoveling snow on a cold day.

_____

_____

_____

You see a little boy crying because he is lost.

_____

_____

_____

Jesus Is Many Things

Unscramble the words to tell about Jesus.

1. When Jesus gave sight to those who could not see, he was a **elhare**. _____

2. When Jesus left Jerusalem with Joseph and Mary, he was a **dogo ons**. _____ _____

3. When Jesus told parables, he was a **ecetahr**.

_____

4. When Jesus loves and cares for us, he is like the **dogo hspehrde**. _____ _____

5. When Simeon saw Jesus in the Temple, he knew that Jesus was the **hsesiMa.** _____

Prayer Service

Leader: Let us begin our prayer with the Sign of the Cross.

A reading from the Book of Psalms.

Know that God created us and watches over us. He cares for us always.

[adapted from Psalm 100:3]

Leader: Let us pray to Jesus.

Jesus, you are the Son of the living God.

All: Receive our thanks and praise.

Leader: Jesus, you are our teacher and friend.

All: Receive our thanks and praise.

Leader: Let us pray together the Lord's Prayer.

Living My Faith

Ways of Being Like Jesus

Jesus cares for all the people in the world. You are like Jesus when you do things to help others.

With My Family

Visit a church that has stained-glass windows. Enjoy the beautiful works of art with your family.

Prayer

Dear God, thank you for giving us Jesus to tell us about your goodness. Help me as I bring your goodness to those I meet today.

My Response

What would you like to thank Jesus for? Draw a picture or write a sentence to thank him.

All Are Welcome

Saint Ignatius of Loyola

Ignatius of Loyola is an important saint.
He learned about Jesus from his family.

Saint Ignatius of Loyola

Ignatius was born in Spain to a large Catholic family. He became a soldier, but he never forgot his Catholic upbringing.

He returned home after being wounded in battle. He read books about Jesus and the saints. Ignatius wanted to be like them. He decided to spend his life doing whatever God wanted of him.

We Worship God

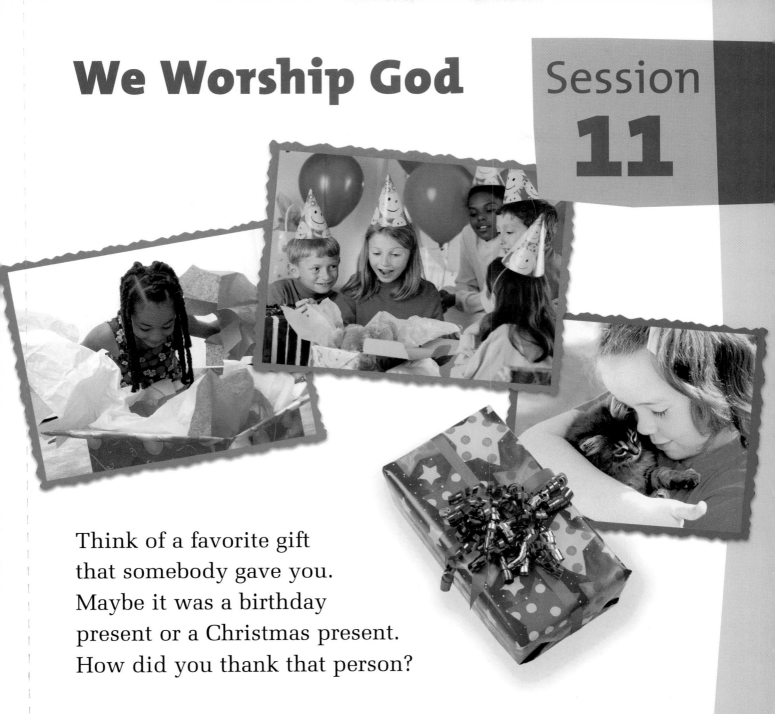

Think of a favorite gift
that somebody gave you.
Maybe it was a birthday
present or a Christmas present.
How did you thank that person?

Prayer

*Jesus, my friend, help me stay close to you so that
I will grow in faith.*

The Apple Orchard

Tiffany and her friend Joey walked through an apple orchard. They looked at the beautiful trees. They talked about how shiny the apples were and about how juicy they must be.

Tiffany noticed some branches on the ground. The farmer had cut these branches from the tree. He cut them because they did not grow fruit. The healthy branches on the trees are like people who choose God. God will help us if we invite him into our lives. We can ask him to guide us.

Jesus Is the Vine

Jesus said, "I am the vine, and my Father is the vine grower. He helps the good branches become healthier. You are already healthy because you have listened to what I said."

Jesus continued, "A branch cannot grow strong unless it stays on the vine. You cannot grow strong unless you stay close to me. Whoever stays close to me will grow strong."

adapted from John 15:1-6

Reading God's Word

The fruit of the Spirit is love, joy, peace, patience, and kindness.

adapted from Galatians 5:22

The Holy Spirit Comes to Us

Jesus gave us the sacraments. They are special signs that God is with us. In the sacraments we receive the Holy Spirit, who brings us God's special gift of grace. This helps us to be God's friends.

The Holy Spirit helps us to act as God wants us to. The good we find in our words or actions is called the **Fruits of the Holy Spirit.** We are able to be kind and loving because God is alive in us.

The Sacrament of Baptism

Baptism is the first sacrament we celebrate. We become children of God and members of the Church when we are baptized. In the **rite** of Baptism, a person is immersed in water or water is poured over the person's head. The grace we receive in the sacraments helps us stay as close to God as the vine is close to the branch.

Baptism takes away **original sin.** This sin is in the world because Adam and Eve chose not to obey God.

Did You Know?

The words of Baptism that the priest says are "I baptize you in the name of the Father, and of the Son, and of the Holy Spirit."

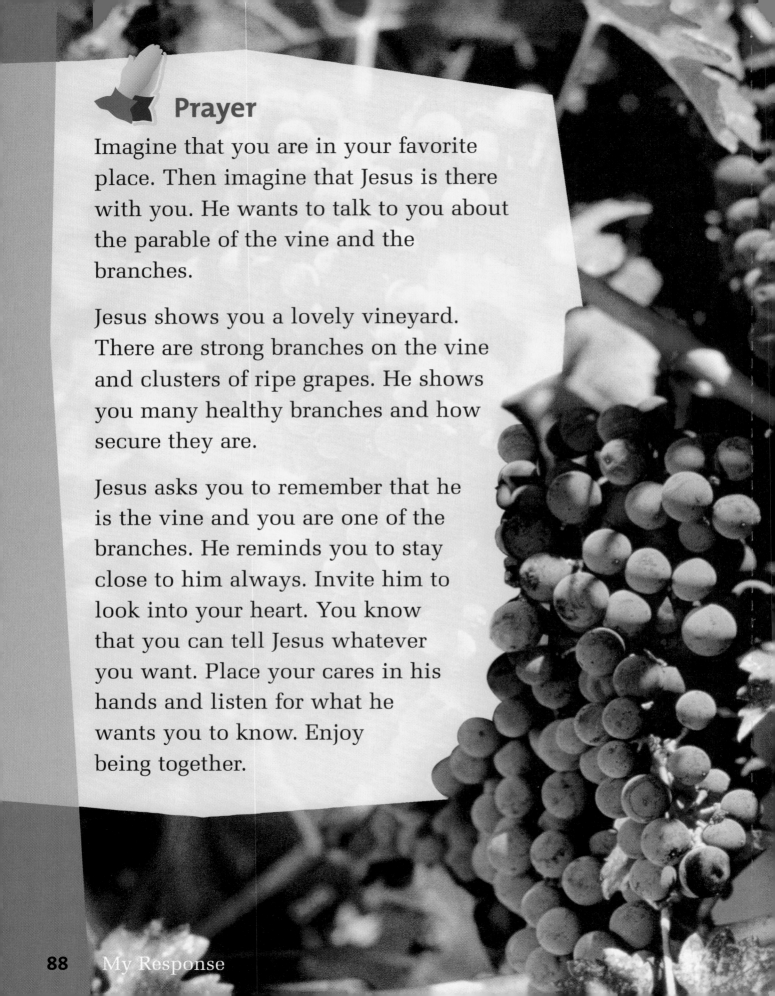

Prayer

Imagine that you are in your favorite place. Then imagine that Jesus is there with you. He wants to talk to you about the parable of the vine and the branches.

Jesus shows you a lovely vineyard. There are strong branches on the vine and clusters of ripe grapes. He shows you many healthy branches and how secure they are.

Jesus asks you to remember that he is the vine and you are one of the branches. He reminds you to stay close to him always. Invite him to look into your heart. You know that you can tell Jesus whatever you want. Place your cares in his hands and listen for what he wants you to know. Enjoy being together.

Faith Summary

Jesus told the parable of the vine to teach us to stay with him. In the sacraments we receive the grace of the Holy Spirit to help us do this.

Help with dinner dishes

Words I Learned

Fruits of the Holy Spirit **original sin** **rite**

Ways of Being Like Jesus

Jesus calls us to act with kindness. You can use kind words. Speak with kindness when you are playing with your friends or family members.

With My Family

Make a chore jar for your family. Have family members pick jobs to do from the jar.

Prayer

Thank you, God, for giving me Jesus. Keep me close as I learn more about you and Jesus, your Son.

My Response

What are some kind words you can use this week? Make a list of three words, phrases, or sentences.

Focus on Faith

God Makes Us His Own

When we send our children to school, we make sure that their possessions are marked so that they can be identified. In ancient times those in power used signet rings to place their seal of authority on documents so that people could identify the document with the authority of the ruler. This is the image the Church uses to help us understand the meaning of the sacraments. In Baptism, Confirmation, and Eucharist we are sealed in the Holy Spirit. These seals identify us as belonging to God. The sacraments form us as God's people, so we can act in service to the world in the way Jesus did.

Dinnertime Conversation Starter

Discuss with your family the various ways in which Jesus served the world. Choose one way your family can effectively continue a specific service that would identify you as Christians.

Our Catholic Heritage

Father James Keller (1900–1977) was a priest who believed that every individual had a contribution to make to society. In 1945 he founded the Christophers, a non-profit organization that uses print and electronic media to spread the message of hope to all people. The motto Father Keller chose for The Christophers is "It is better to light one candle than to curse the darkness." The Christophers' work continues today with weekly television and radio programs, a daily radio message, newspaper columns, and brochures that provide resources for facing difficult life issues. You can find more information about the Christophers and their work at **www.christophers.org**.

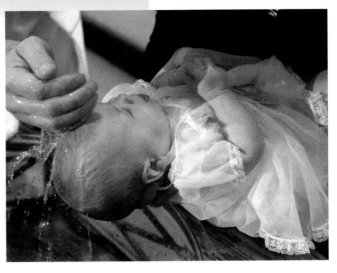

Hints for at Home

Help your child nurture an ivy plant in your home. You will need an ivy plant, a clay pot, potting soil, paints or permanent markers, a watering can, and pruning shears.

Have your child decorate the clay pot, using the paints. Ask him or her to write *I am the vine* on the pot. Then plant the ivy in it. Water the plant regularly and invite your child to observe what happens over time. Show your child how to pull away leaves that become dried out. Use the pruning shears to show what occurs when you clip off a section of dead growth. (New growth takes place.) Relate this growth to the parable of the vine.

Focus on Prayer

Your child has reflected on the parable of the vine and on the security and comfort of knowing that Jesus holds us close to himself. Share with your child a moment when you felt Jesus was with you.

Celebrating Reconciliation

Has a friend ever been unkind to you? Think of how it hurt your friendship. How did you become friends again?

 Prayer

Jesus, my Savior, help me be aware of my sins.
Teach me to ask for forgiveness when I am wrong.

Zaccheus the Rich Man

Zaccheus was a dishonest tax collector. He was very rich. One day he heard that Jesus was coming through town. Zaccheus wanted to see Jesus very much. But Jesus was walking in a big crowd and Zaccheus was not tall. He could not see over the crowd.

Zaccheus ran ahead and climbed up a tree. Jesus saw him and said, "Zaccheus, come down. I want to stay at your house today." This made Zaccheus very happy.

The people in the crowd became angry. They wondered why Jesus was going to the home of a sinner.

Zacchaeus said to Jesus, "I will give half of everything I have to the poor. I will give money back to anyone I have cheated."

Jesus was pleased. He said that Zacchaeus was saved that day.

adapted from Luke 19:2-9

Reading God's Word

Sell what you have and give to those who do not have much. Your treasure is with the Lord. No thief can steal that from you.

adapted from Luke 12:33

Making Peace With God

We choose to turn away from God when we sin. We turn away from God when we commit a **mortal sin** or a **venial sin.**

Mortal sin is a very serious wrong. Venial sin is a less serious wrong. All sin hurts our relationship with God and others.

Sin is forgiven when we celebrate the **Sacrament of Penance.** In **confession** we tell God we are sorry. **Contrition** is the name given to the sadness we feel when we know we have sinned. In **reconciliation** we make peace with God and with others. We promise God that we will try not to sin again.

 Link to Liturgy

Near the beginning of Mass, we pray special prayers to ask for God's forgiveness and mercy.

Before going to confession it is important to make an **examination of conscience.** This will help us think about anything we have said or done that has hurt our friendship with God and with others. Your conscience will help you know if you have done something wrong.

Jesus was happy that Zacchaeus was sorry about cheating so many people. Jesus will be happy with you when you come to him in confession and tell him you are sorry for your sins. He will always forgive you.

God and You

Look at the words in dark type on these two pages, in the Making Peace With God section. Which of those words name ways to improve your relationship with God? Circle those. Which ones name things that harm your relationship with God? Underline those.

Prayer

God wants us to be sorry for our sins and to ask for his forgiveness. We pray a special prayer to tell him we are sorry for having sinned. We ask God to help us avoid sinning in the future.

Act of Contrition

My God,
I am sorry for my sins with all my heart.
In choosing to do wrong
and failing to do good,
I have sinned against you
whom I should love above all things.
I firmly intend, with your help,
to do penance,
to sin no more,
and to avoid whatever
  leads me to sin.
Our Savior Jesus Christ
suffered and
died for us.
In his name,
  my God,
  have mercy.

Amen

Faith Summary

Zacchaeus opened his heart to Jesus. Our sins can be forgiven through the Sacrament of Penance.

Words I Learned

confession   contrition
examination of conscience   mortal sin
reconciliation   Sacrament of Penance   venial sin

Ways of Being Like Jesus

Jesus treated all people the same. You are like Jesus when you do good things for relatives and classmates.

With My Family

Welcome people by creating a Welcome sign to put in your home.

Prayer

Thank you, Jesus, for helping me to forgive others as you forgive me.

My Response

Have you treated someone badly? What steps can you take to apologize?

Focus on Faith

Jesus Dines With Zacchaeus

When our children hurt one another, we can feel discouraged. We know that even though apologies are given and accepted, resentment can remain. Luke presents an account of reconciliation in the story of Zacchaeus, a tax collector whom people hated. Jesus did not scold Zacchaeus when they met, but rather asked Zacchaeus to invite him to dinner. Jesus' eating with Zacchaeus meant that Jesus forgave him and accepted him. Zacchaeus responded by vowing to pay back everyone he had cheated. Jesus teaches us that we can help our children be reconciled with God and with one another. The family dinner gives us the opportunity to share conversation and build relationships.

Dinnertime Conversation Starter

Arrange a time to invite to dinner someone with whom your family needs to rebuild a relationship.

Spirituality in Action

Your child is learning about reconciliation. Remind your child that we also pray for reconciliation among groups of people. Explain that criticizing others because of their appearance, religious beliefs, or way of life is not appropriate and is hurtful to them and to God. Encourage your child to get to know those who may be from other cultures or backgrounds.

Hints for at Home

Create walk-in-peace footprints for the entryway to each bedroom in your home. Make one pair for each room. You will need poster board, markers, scissors, and double-sided tape. Have your child trace his or her feet on the poster board once for every bedroom in your home. Decorate the outlines and write *Walk in peace* on them. Cut out the outlines. Use the tape to attach one pair to the floor outside each bedroom door, facing out from the bedroom.

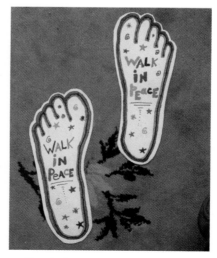

out from the bedroom. Remind your family members to walk in peace as they leave their bedrooms each morning.

Focus on Prayer

Your child is learning to pray the Act of Contrition. Pray it with your child at bedtime after he or she reviews the good and hurtful things that were done that day.

The Sacrament of Penance

Sometimes we do or say something to hurt others.
How can we make it up to them?

 Prayer

*Jesus, my friend, teach me about your forgiveness so
that I may learn to make peace with God and others.*

Jesus Heals

Jesus was talking with some people in a house. The people crowded the rooms and blocked the doorways.

Four men walked by carrying their friend. Their friend wanted to see Jesus. He was paralyzed and could not walk. The men climbed to the roof of the house and made an opening. They lowered their friend to Jesus.

Jesus saw their faith. He said to the man who was paralyzed, "Your sins are forgiven."

Some people in the crowd were surprised. They said, "Only God can forgive sins!"

Jesus told the people that he had the power to forgive sins. Then he turned to the man who was paralyzed and said, "Stand up and walk home." The man got up and walked away. The people were amazed. They knew that Jesus must be God.

adapted from Mark 2:1-12

Following the Story

Number the pictures in the order that they happened in the story.

Jesus Forgives

Jesus forgave the sins of the man who could not walk. He forgives our sins too. Today Jesus does this through the priests who forgive our sins in his name.

Our sins are forgiven as the priest extends his hands over us and prays the prayer of **absolution.** The prayer ends with the words "May God grant you pardon and peace and I absolve you from your sins in the name of the Father, and of the Son, and of the Holy Spirit."

Reading God's Word

The people are given knowledge that they are saved because their sins have been forgiven.

adapted from Luke 1:77

After we have confessed our sins, the priest gives us a **penance.** This is a prayer or a deed we do to make up for our sins. We tell God we want to live as his children.

The grace we receive in the Sacrament of Penance will strengthen us when we are tempted to sin. It will help us avoid sin and grow closer to God.

We leave confession knowing that we are at peace with God and with others.

 Did You Know?

The priest must keep absolutely secret the sins that people have confessed to him. This is called the seal of confession.

Prayer

Contrition is the sadness we feel when we know we have sinned. We pray an Act of Contrition to tell God that we are sorry.

God wants us to make peace with him. He wants us to make peace with others. We ask forgiveness when we do something that is wrong.

Jesus knows what is in your heart. Know that you are safe with him. Be still and spend some time with Jesus. Listen to what Jesus wants you to know.

Faith Summary

When we celebrate the Sacrament of Penance, our sins are forgiven. We make peace with God and with others.

Words I Learned

absolution   penance

Ways of Being Like Jesus

Jesus worked to bring people together. Be a peacemaker with your family and friends.

With My Family

This week forgive a family member or ask someone to forgive you.

Prayer

Thank you, God, my Father, for forgiving me. Help me to be a more peaceful child of yours.

My Response

How will you be a peacemaker this week? Write a sentence to explain your idea.

Focus on Faith

Jesus Forgives Us

The Gospel of Mark tells the story of the man who was paralyzed and could not reach Jesus. His friends helped him by carrying him to the top of the house where Jesus was staying, tearing open the thatched roof, and lowering the man's pallet. Jesus first forgave his sins and then told him to take up his pallet and walk. The man had dependable friends who helped him reach Jesus. Jesus helps us when we recognize our need to be forgiven of our sins. He has given us the Sacrament of Penance through which we can confess to a priest and receive absolution. Once we are forgiven and reconciled with God and one another, we can face the future with hope.

The Healing of the Paralytic, from the Manuscript of The Four Gospels

Dinnertime Conversation Starter

Like the man who was paralyzed, we often have trouble getting close to Jesus. Help your child talk about what he or she can do to stay close to Jesus.

Spirituality in Action

Your child is learning that through the Sacrament of Penance we make peace with God and others. He or she is learning

that God wants us to be reconciled with members of our community and our world. Notice words or actions that prevent peace or that build "walls" between people. Discuss with your child small steps that he or she might take to be a peacemaker.

Focus on Prayer

Your child was encouraged to live in peace. Pray with your child for a spirit of peace and forgiveness at home.

Hints for at Home

To remind your family that we can receive forgiveness for our sins, make healing bandages to use in your home. You will need plastic bandages of various sizes and shapes, permanent markers, and small stickers.

Invite your child to write messages, such as *God is with me* or *Live in peace,* on the bandages with the markers. Decorate the bandages with the stickers. Use the bandages each time a skinned knee or cut finger needs care.

Mary Shows Us the Way

When do you need help with something in your life? Is there a subject in school that is difficult? Who usually helps you?

Prayer

God, my Heavenly Father, teach me about Mary so that I may learn to follow her example.

Mary Visits Elizabeth

The angel Gabriel told Mary that she was going to be the mother of Jesus. Soon after that, Mary went to visit her cousin Elizabeth.

Elizabeth was very happy to see Mary. She praised Mary for her love of God. She called her blessed.

Mary said to Elizabeth, "God is great. He is my Savior. All people will call me blessed. God has done great things for me."

Then Mary said, "God's name is holy. His mercy will last forever."

adapted from Luke 1:39-55

These words that Mary used to praise God have become a special prayer. Catholics call this prayer the **Magnificat.**

 Did You Know?

Catholics around the world honor Mary.

Poem of Praise

You should praise God as Mary did. Use the words in the box to complete this poem of praise.

Jesus	name	way

Mary praised God,

And we do the same,

For he is our Savior,

And holy is his _____.

Through actions and words,

Mary shows us the _____

To share God's great love,

With one another each day.

If we obey God,

As Mary shows us,

We stay with the Father

And his Son, _____.

Mother of the Church

Like Mary, the Church has a special relationship with God.

The Church is made up of people who are called by God. The Church shows the world how much God loves them. God loves everyone.

Mary is the Mother of the Church. She received God's help so she could follow him.

God gives us the same help, or grace. Mary prays for us so that we will listen to God.

Reading God's Word

Mary remembered all these things and kept them always in her heart.

adapted from Luke 2:19

Prayer

Mary had the courage and love to do what God asked her to do. In your imagination go to Mary and talk with her about saying yes to God. Ask her what it was like for her to do this.

Tell her it is not always easy for you to say yes to God. Stay with Mary for a while. Pray together to God to help you say yes too.

Faith Summary

Elizabeth called Mary blessed. We honor Mary in a special prayer called the Magnificat.

Word I Learned

Magnificat

Ways of Being Like Jesus

Jesus loved his mother very much. You are like Jesus when you honor Mary.

With My Family

Talk with family members about ways to honor Mary in your home.

Living My Faith

Prayer

Thank you, God, for the example of Mary. Help me say yes to you.

My Response

What can you do this week to show your love for Mary, our Mother?

Focus on Faith

Supporting One Another

We all need the help of others to become the people God wants us to be. After Mary said yes to becoming the mother of Jesus, she received love and support from her cousin Elizabeth. When Elizabeth saw Mary, Elizabeth shouted in joy and considered herself blessed that Mary came to visit her. Mary responded in joy with the Magnificat, her song of thanks to God. Elizabeth affirmed Mary and supported her faith in God. In the same way, we are called to support one another's faith. As parents we have the special responsibility to support our children's faith. We begin doing this by creating a positive environment in which their faith can grow.

Incontro di Maria, Mariotto Albertinelli

Dinnertime Conversation Starter

Conduct a mental treasure hunt with your family. One by one, picture the rooms in your home. Are there statues, pictures, books, or crosses that identify your home as Catholic? What can be done to create a more Catholic environment?

Spirituality in Action

Mary provides us with an example of how God loves the less fortunate in a special way. He looked beyond "his handmaid's lowliness" and lifted her up. When we assist the poor, we are acting as God calls us to act. Anything we do for them, we do for God. With your child establish a special box containing items that your family can donate to a shelter in your community. Place things such as mittens, hats, socks, toothpaste, toys, and books into the box and donate the contents from time to time throughout the year.

In Our Parish

With your pastor's permission ask families to decorate bulletin boards in the church to honor Mary. Families might work together to create small works of art to show their reverence for Mary.

Focus on Prayer

Your child has reflected on Luke 1:46–55, which contains the words of the Magnificat. Mary praised God for the great things he had done for her. Talk with your child about ways in which God has blessed your family.

Review

Through the Church we are part of a community. The sacraments keep us close to God and to one another.

Prayer

Jesus, my model of goodness, guide me to seek forgiveness for my sins so that I may remain close to you.

Faith Summary

Jesus shared the parable of the vine to remind us that he wants us to remain close to him. Jesus comes to us in the sacraments.

Jesus forgave Zacchaeus his sins. He became a friend to Zacchaeus. Jesus does the same for us in the Sacrament of Penance.

The Church celebrates the Sacrament of Penance with us. When we celebrate the sacrament, we make peace with God and one another.

Mary shows us how to say yes to God.

Keeping God Close

Color and cut out the wristband. Tie it on.

God Is Great

Vocabulary Word Puzzle

Fill in the missing letters to spell words you learned in Unit 3. Use the words to complete the sentences below.

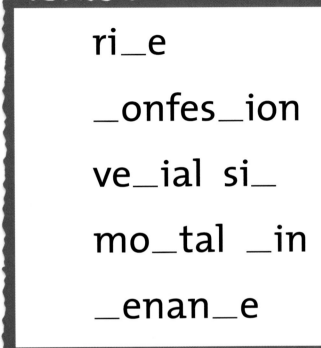

ri_e

_onfes_ion

ve_ial si_

mo_tal _in

_enan_e

1. You completely turn your back on God if you commit a _____ _____.

2. Water may be poured over a person's head in the _____ of Baptism.

3. We tell God we are sorry in the Sacrament of _____.

4. Sins are forgiven in _____.

5. A _____ _____ is a less serious wrong.

God's Community

God is happy when we work together to be part of his community, the Church. He is happy when we remember that we are his children.

Bring God's Children Together

Color the letters and cut out the boxes.
Unscramble the letters. What do they spell?

Prayer Service

Leader: We praise God by reading his word.

A reading from the Book of Psalms.

Have mercy on me, God, in your goodness; wash away my guilt; keep me from sinning.

[adapted from Psalm 51:3-4]

Leader: We can praise Mary and ask her to help us. After each phrase, say "pray for us."

Mary, model of obedience,
Mary, mother of Jesus,
Mary, full of grace,
Mary, blessed among women,
Mary, full of love,

Let us pray the Hail Mary together.

Living My Faith

Ways of Being Like Jesus

Jesus offers forgiveness to those who are hurting. You are like Jesus when you choose to forgive others.

With My Family

Talk about how Jesus helped everybody. Tell family members you are sorry if you treat them in an unkind way.

Prayer

Loving Jesus, thank you for helping me to be sorry for my sins. Help me to become a more forgiving person.

My Response

Mary will ask God to help us. What would you like Mary to ask God for you?

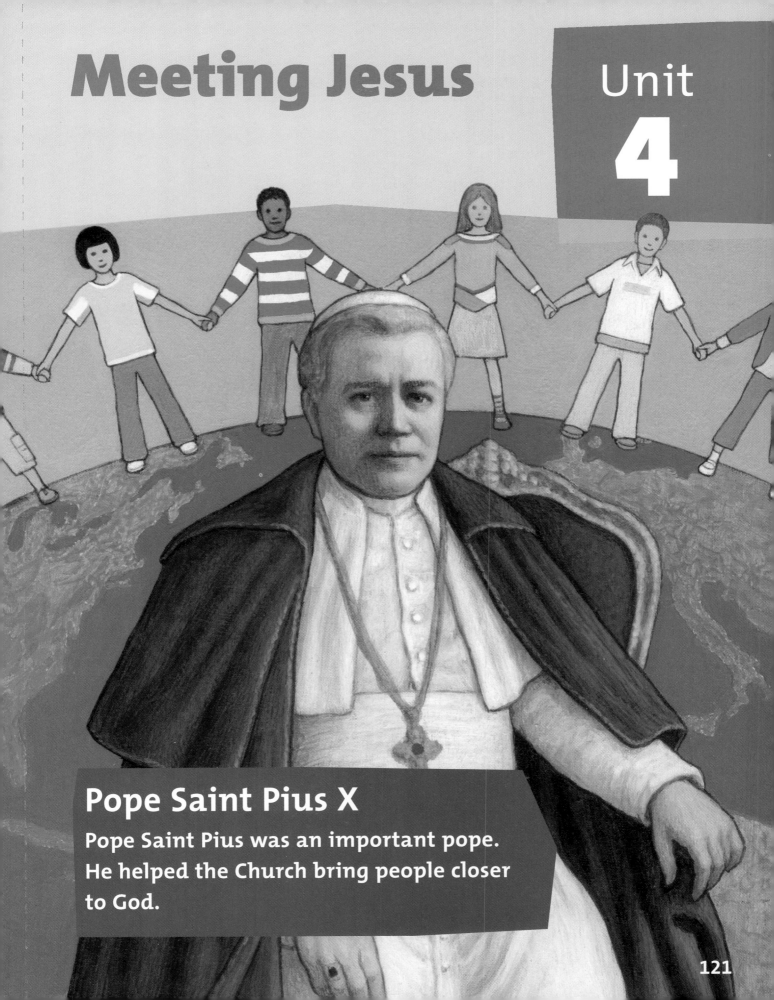

Meeting Jesus

Pope Saint Pius X

Pope Saint Pius was an important pope. He helped the Church bring people closer to God.

Pope Saint Pius X

Pius X wanted Catholics to receive Holy Communion often. He believed that children should be able to receive Holy Communion around age seven. He wanted them to be close to Jesus.

Pope Pius X spread God's love to the world. He spent his life helping others. He created charities to care for people who were poor.

New Life in Jesus

Have you ever been a member of a group? Are you part of a choir or a sports team? What are the good things about being a member of a group?

Prayer

Jesus, my friend, help me learn about the sacraments so that I may appreciate what you are giving me.

Peter Speaks to the People

Jesus chose Peter to lead the Church. He wanted Peter to keep showing people how to be close to God.

Peter said to the people, "Change your lives and be baptized in the name of Jesus Christ. Then your sins will be forgiven. You will receive the gift of the Holy Spirit."

adapted from Acts of the Apostles 2:38

Did You Know?

Vatican City is the home of the pope. It is located in Italy.

Special Signs From God

A sacrament is a special sign. It shows that God is with us. Sacraments were given to the Church by Jesus.

The **Sacraments of Initiation** are Baptism, **Confirmation,** and **Eucharist.** These sacraments bring us into God's family. They give us grace. Grace is a gift we receive from God.

Baptism

Baptism is the beginning of our new life with Jesus. We are saved from our sins in Baptism. Baptism gives us sanctifying grace. This is the gift of God's new life in us.

We become a member of the Church when we are baptized. We become part of God's family.

Confirmation

Confirmation makes us stronger in faith. It helps us become better Christians. God's sanctifying grace does this for us.

Eucharist

We receive the **Body and Blood of Christ** in the Eucharist. This is called **Holy Communion.**

The bread and wine of the Eucharist become the Body and Blood of Christ. This happens through the words of **consecration** prayed by the priest.

 Reading God's Word

The Spirit says, "Come." Whoever is thirsty may come forward and receive life-giving water.

adapted from Revelation 22:17

A Walk on the Beach

As Andre was walking on the beach, he thought about the important words he was learning. Draw a line to lead Andre from these words to the clues that describe them. The first one is done for you.

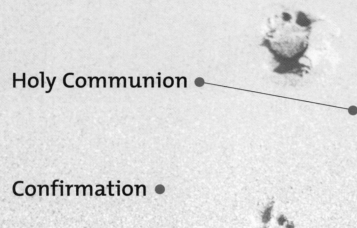

Holy Communion •————————• The Body and Blood of Christ, which we receive in the Eucharist

Confirmation • • Sacrament in which the bread and wine become the Body and Blood of Christ

Sacraments of Initiation • • Makes us stronger in faith

Eucharist • • Baptism, Confirmation, and Eucharist

Baptism • 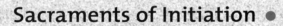 • The beginning of our new life with Jesus

Prayer

We know that God gave us water to drink because we need it to live.

Think about the many things you can do with water. Maybe you like to go swimming or make water balloons. You can take a long, cool drink of water on a hot day. What other things do you do with water?

Now think about the water that was poured over you when you were baptized. You were given new life with Jesus. You became part of God's family. In your imagination meet Jesus in your favorite place. Tell him how happy you are to be God's child. Listen with your heart to what he tells you.

Faith Summary

Baptism, Confirmation, and Eucharist are the Sacraments of Initiation.

Words I Learned

Body and Blood of Christ
consecration
Holy Communion

Confirmation
Eucharist
Sacraments of Initiation

Ways of Being Like Jesus

You are like Jesus when you do good deeds for neighbors and others.

With My Family

As a family, volunteer your time or money to a charity.

 Prayer

Thank you, God, for your gift of grace. Help me to always stay close to you.

My Response

Jesus came to serve you.
How can you serve others?

a parent page

Focus on Faith

New Life in God

From the window of their house, the mother and her children could see a pair of birds building a new nest. As time passed, they could see tiny eggs in the nest and the careful way they were kept warm. They noticed how the birds chirped in warning if an animal came too close. Then tiny birds came out of their shells. As spring turned into summer, the tiny birds grew and learned how to fly. One day they were gone, leaving the empty nest behind. Nature has many examples of life's transitions. As Christians, we celebrate these transitions in our spiritual lives in the sacraments. The sacraments that bring us new life in God are Baptism, Confirmation, and Eucharist.

Dinnertime Conversation Starter

What significant transitions or changes are your family facing? Explain to your child how the sacraments will provide the grace to help the family cope with these changes.

Hints for at Home

With your child create a "Jesus, Light My Way" switch-plate cover for a light switch. You will need a plain switch-plate cover, a permanent marker, and stickers, sequins, and other decorative items. Have your child use the marker to write *Jesus, light my way* on the switch-plate cover. Then have him or her use the stickers, sequins, and other items to decorate the plate. Attach the completed plate in a prominent room in your home.

Spirituality in Action

Jesus lived a life of service. Guide your child to find new ways to help others. Begin a family service project for the children's ward of a local hospital. With your family create placemats to deliver to the children there. You will need cardboard, scissors, fabric, glue, construction paper, permanent markers, and clear adhesive or laminate covering. Use the cardboard to form the bottom of the placemat. Cut the fabric to fit over the cardboard and glue it on top of the cardboard. Then write cheerful greetings on the construction paper and glue it to the fabric. Place the clear covering over the top of the placemat. Deliver the finished products to the children's ward.

Focus on Prayer

Share with your child the story of his or her Baptism. Look at photos or videos of the Baptism and explain how you felt on the day they were taken. With your child praise Jesus for the new life he gives us.

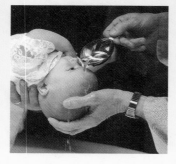

Jesus Loves the Church

Imagine that a new child has moved into your neighborhood. How can you welcome your new neighbor? What can you do to make him or her feel at home?

 Prayer

Jesus, my friend, help me welcome you into my heart and my life. Help me do good for others.

Inviting Jesus to Dinner

After Jesus died, two of his **disciples** were walking along a road. They met a man. The disciples did not know who he was. The disciples told him about all that had happened to Jesus. They invited the man to join them for dinner.

The man sat down with the disciples at the dinner table. He broke bread, blessed it, and gave it to them. When he did this, they knew that he was Jesus. They knew that Jesus had risen.

adapted from Luke 24:13-31

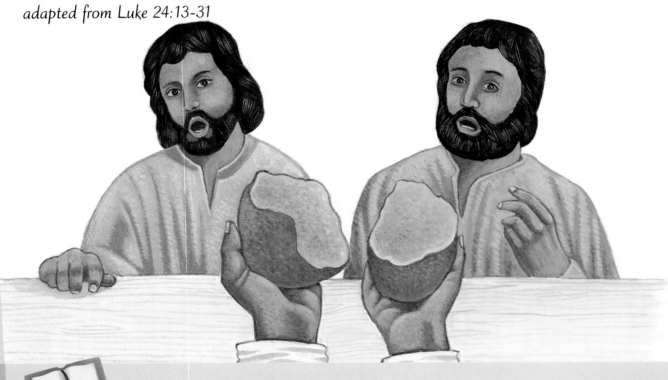

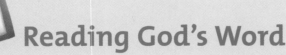 **Reading God's Word**

Jesus' followers came together to learn, to pray, and to break bread.

adapted from Acts of the Apostles 2:42

A Message for Jesus

Like the disciples in the story, you can invite
Jesus into your life. Imagine that Jesus is coming
to visit your home. Welcome him by writing
a message on the stairway. Write one word on
each step.

Welcoming Jesus

The Holy Spirit comes to us in Baptism and stays with us throughout our lives. Every day the grace of the Holy Spirit helps us to love others. When we love others, we welcome Jesus into our lives.

The most important way we remember that Jesus is with us is in the celebration of the Eucharist or the **Sacrifice of the Mass.** The Mass helps us remember that Jesus died for us and saved us from our sins.

Welcome to Mass

Devin sat between his mother and sister. He waited quietly for Mass to begin. Devin felt close to his family and close to God at Mass.

Devin saw a new student from his class. Her name was Nikki. Devin and his family invited Nikki's family to sit with them. They made Nikki's family feel welcome.

In many parishes there are people who welcome others to the church. Sometimes family members share in this **ministry**.

Link to Liturgy

Many churches have ministers of hospitality who welcome people to the parish church for Mass.

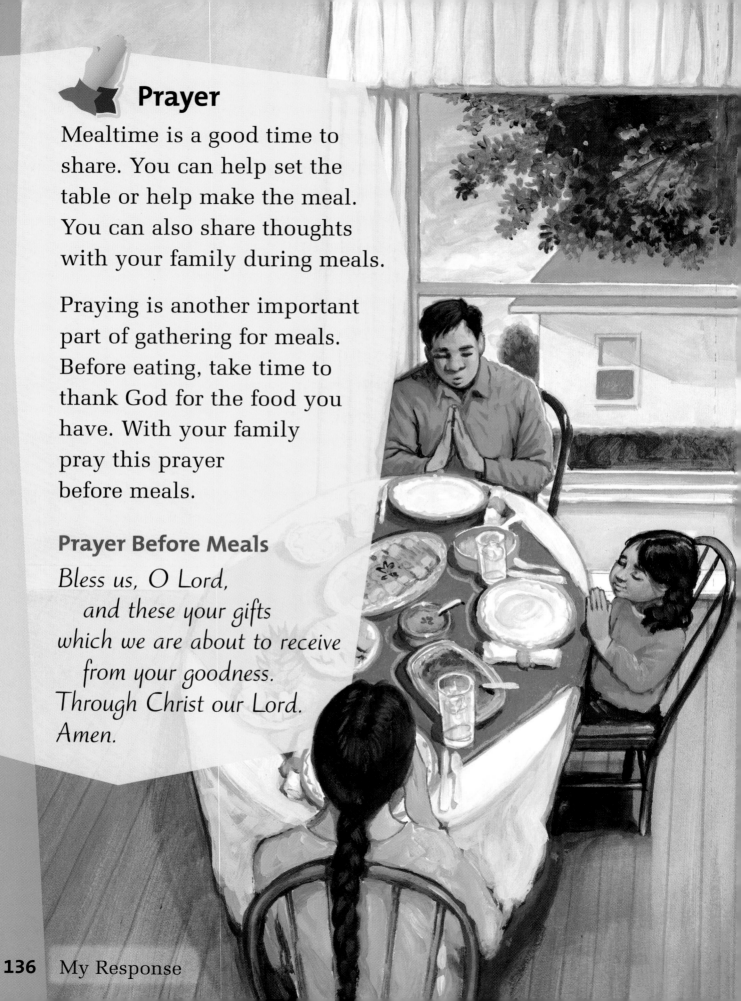

Prayer

Mealtime is a good time to share. You can help set the table or help make the meal. You can also share thoughts with your family during meals.

Praying is another important part of gathering for meals. Before eating, take time to thank God for the food you have. With your family pray this prayer before meals.

Prayer Before Meals

Bless us, O Lord,
 and these your gifts
which we are about to receive
 from your goodness.
Through Christ our Lord.
Amen.

Faith Summary

The Holy Spirit comes to us in the sacraments. His grace helps us love Jesus and others. At Mass we remember that Jesus died to save us from our sins.

Words I Learned

disciple   ministry   Sacrifice of the Mass

Ways of Being Like Jesus

Jesus welcomed new people into his life. You are like Jesus when you welcome new students at school.

With My Family

As a family, take a treat to a new neighbor.

 ## Prayer

Loving Jesus, you are always welcome in my life. Help me to welcome others.

My Response

Draw a picture to show how you can help a new person in your school, neighborhood, or parish.

Focus on Faith

Welcoming Jesus Into Our Lives

The young boy could not help but notice that his friend was not available to play on Sunday mornings. When he asked, he discovered that the family went to Sunday Mass. Intrigued, the boy asked his parents' permission to attend Mass with his friend's family. His parents agreed, and he attended Mass with the family regularly. The young boy was attracted to the faith through the hospitality of his friend's family. The story of the two disciples walking with Jesus after the Resurrection is also a story of hospitality. At the end of the walk, the disciples asked Jesus to dine with them, welcoming him into their lives. *(Luke 24:13–35)*

Supper at Emmaus, Ivo Dulcic

Dinnertime Conversation Starter

Discuss ways in which your family can welcome people into your lives.

Hints for at Home

Development of children's sacramental living starts at home, and a parent's blessing each day can play a big part in fostering this development. For example, you can express yourself in a loving manner when greeting your child or saying goodbye. You can also teach your

children to greet others in a Christian manner. With your child bake a loaf of bread, using a favorite recipe. At a family meal ask your child to serve as a minister of hospitality and help your family members to their seats. Then cut a piece of bread for each member of the family. Invite each person to say a blessing and pass a piece to the person seated at his or her right. Conclude by praying as a group, "Let us remember Jesus, the bread of life."

Our Catholic Heritage

Vatican II gave us the Rite of Christian Initiation of Adults, or RCIA, which describes how the Church

helps those who are searching for God. With God's help many adults enter the way of faith and conversion as the Holy Spirit opens their hearts.

Every Holy Saturday thousands of men and women celebrate the Sacraments of Initiation—Baptism, Confirmation, and Eucharist. They become new members of the Catholic Church through these sacraments.

Focus on Prayer

Your child has reflected on the story of two of Jesus' disciples who recognized him during the course of a meal. Also, your child has learned the Prayer Before Meals. Use this simple mealtime prayer. You may wish to expand on it by asking the members of your family to add a word of personal thanks. The words to this prayer can be found at www.FindingGod.org.

Gathering for Mass

Have you ever invited friends to a sleepover? What did you have to do to get ready for them? Was it exciting to prepare for this fun time?

 Prayer

God, my Father, help me discover the many ways I can praise you and ask for your blessings at Mass.

The Mass Begins

The O'Malley family attends Mass every Sunday and on special days. Mrs. O'Malley is a reader, so she sits near the front of the church with her family.

Mrs. Li leads everyone in singing the entrance song. Father Diego comes to the altar during the song. He greets the people. Then everyone prays that God will forgive their sins.

Next, the Gloria is prayed. This prayer gives glory to God the Father, and Jesus, his Son, and the Holy Spirit.

Hearing God's Message

Mrs. O'Malley walks to the place where she will read. This is the **ambo.** She will read Bible stories for everyone from a special book. It is called the **Lectionary.**

"You have known about God's messages since you were a child. These messages help you realize what is important."

adapted from 2 Timothy 3: 14-17

Then Father Diego goes to the ambo to read a story about Jesus' life. After this, Father Diego explains how all of the readings have an important message for our daily lives. This is called the **homily.**

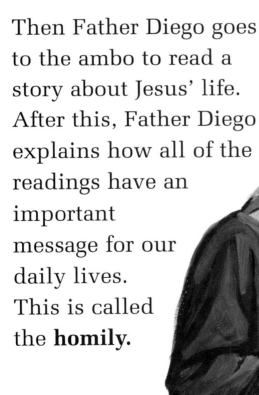

Responding to God's Word

After the homily the people express their belief in the teachings of the Church. They do this by saying, "I believe."

The Bible readings and the homily are part of the **Liturgy of the Word.** This is the time in the Mass when we listen to God's Word from the Bible. The Liturgy of the Word ends when the people pray together for those in need of their prayers.

Reading God's Word

The word of the Lord will last forever.

adapted from Psalm 119:89

The First Part of the Mass

Below are parts of the Mass that you have read about. They are in a jumbled order. Write numbers in the spaces to show the correct order.

_____The priest reads a story about Jesus' life.

_____The people say "I believe" to the teachings of the Church.

_____The priest explains the readings in the homily.

_____The people pray the Gloria, a prayer praising God.

_____The people pray to God to help those in need.

_____The people sing as the priest comes to the altar.

_____A reader reads stories from the Bible.

 Link to Liturgy

We are asked to respond to each reading during the Liturgy of the Word. When the reader says "The Word of the Lord," we say, "Thanks be to God."

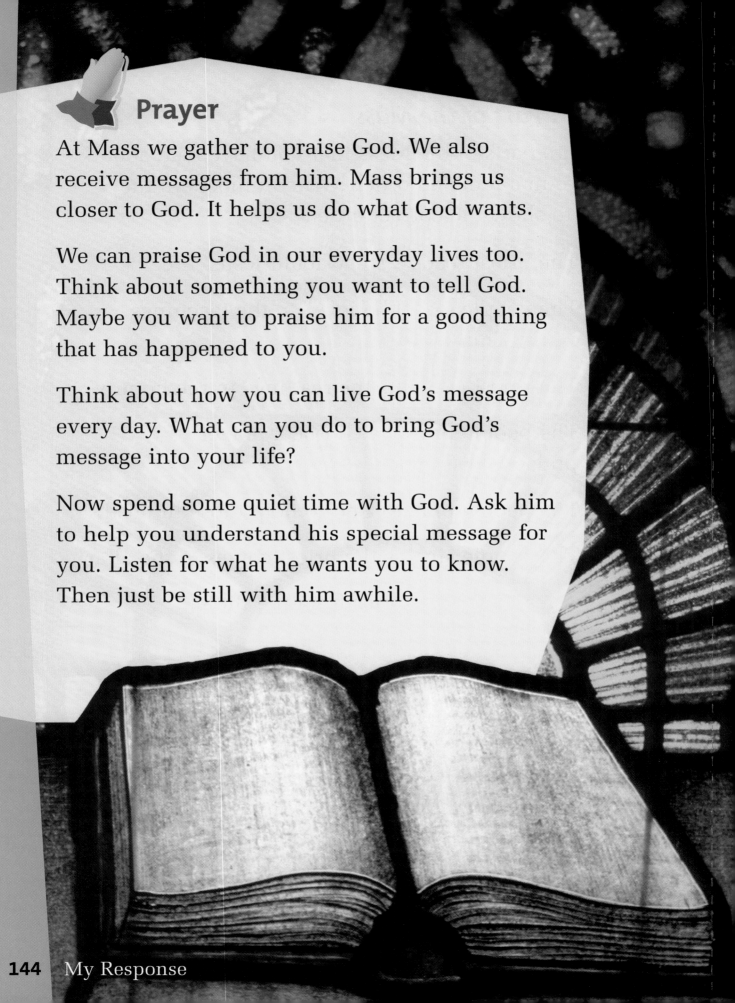

Prayer

At Mass we gather to praise God. We also receive messages from him. Mass brings us closer to God. It helps us do what God wants.

We can praise God in our everyday lives too. Think about something you want to tell God. Maybe you want to praise him for a good thing that has happened to you.

Think about how you can live God's message every day. What can you do to bring God's message into your life?

Now spend some quiet time with God. Ask him to help you understand his special message for you. Listen for what he wants you to know. Then just be still with him awhile.

Faith Summary

At Mass we praise God and ask for his blessing. The readings make Jesus present to us in a special way.

Words I Learned

ambo   homily   Lectionary

Liturgy of the Word

Ways of Being Like Jesus

You are like Jesus when your actions show that God is with you.

With My Family

As a family, greet the priest after Mass.

 Prayer

Thank you, Jesus, for giving us your message. Help me listen carefully. I want to follow you.

My Response

Make a list of people you want to pray for. Take it with you the next time you go to Mass.

Focus on Faith

Jesus Is With Us

The little boy asked his mother whether it was true that God is inside us. She answered yes. Later she heard her son walking around the dining room table. "What are you doing?" she asked. "I am giving God a ride," he answered. A few moments later she heard him running around the table. When she asked, "What are you doing now?" he answered, "I am giving God a fast ride!" Our children have a wonderful sense of God in their lives. Attending Sunday Mass gives them the opportunity to hear God's word in the Scripture readings, to share songs of faith with their parish community, and to discover friends in faithful families. The people of their community keep God alive in their hearts.

Dinnertime Conversation Starter

Does your family have a special Sunday routine—Mass and a bike ride, Mass and a visit with grandma, Mass and a big breakfast? Discuss ways that you and your family can make the Lord's day special.

Hints for at Home

Read these Scripture passages with your child. Discuss what Jesus wants us to learn from them.

"Let the children come to me. Do not prevent them, because the kingdom of God belongs to them."

adapted from Mark 10:14

"Jesus spoke to them again, saying, 'I am the light of the world. Whoever follows me will not walk in darkness, but will have the light of life.'"

John 8:12

"Pray without ceasing."

1 Thessalonians 5:17

Spirituality in Action

Create a special bulletin board or a place on the refrigerator to post prayer intentions. Encourage family members to think of friends, neighbors, and others who need their prayers. When you go to Mass, take along your special intentions and offer them to God.

Focus on Prayer

Your child has started to learn the parts of the Mass. In this session your child has been introduced to the Liturgy of the Word: entrance, Gloria, readings, homily, and general intercessions. The next time you go to Mass, help your child identify the different parts of the Liturgy of the Word. Lead him or her to respond "Thanks be to God" when the lector says "The Word of the Lord."

Celebrating the Eucharist

Have you ever given something to a friend? Have you shared something special with a relative? How did giving and sharing bring you closer to them?

 Prayer

Jesus, my Savior, help me share your love with others.

The Last Supper

Jesus sat at the table with his disciples. He said, "I want to share this supper with you."

Then Jesus took the bread. He blessed it and broke it. He gave it to them and said, "This is my body, which will be given for you. Do this in memory of me."

After the meal he took a cup of wine. He said, "This is my blood. It is given for you."

adapted from Luke 22:14-20

 Reading God's Word

Jesus sacrificed himself for our sins. He is with God forever.

adapted from Hebrews 10:12

Liturgy of the Eucharist

Suki and her family go to Mass together every Sunday. Last week as the **Liturgy of the Eucharist** began, they brought the gifts of bread and wine to the priest at the **altar.** Suki and her family listened as the priest asked God to accept and bless the gifts.

During the consecration the priest repeated the words of Jesus at the Last Supper. The bread and wine became the Body and Blood of Christ. The priest invited everyone to pray the Lord's Prayer and to share a sign of peace. Soon it was time to receive Holy Communion.

When the Liturgy of the Eucharist was over, the priest blessed everyone with the Sign of the Cross. He told them to do good works and to praise God for his goodness to them.

Did You Know?

Sunday is special because it is the Lord's day.

Our Most Important Prayer

The Mass is the most important way that Catholics pray. It is so special that Mass is celebrated every day. As Catholics, we should attend Mass every Sunday. The Church wants us to receive Holy Communion at every Mass we attend.

The Church also wants us to attend Mass on **Holy Days of Obligation.** These are days when we go to Mass to remember great things God has done for us.

Sharing Jesus' Love

Jesus shares the wonderful gift of himself in the Eucharist. We can follow Jesus' loving example by sharing ourselves with others. All of these pictures show examples of sharing.

Mark the two examples that you think are the best. Under these pictures write a sentence explaining why you think they are the best examples of sharing.

_____

_____

_____

_____

_____

_____

_____

_____

Prayer

The Liturgy of the Eucharist helps prepare us to receive Jesus. The priest says, "This is the Lamb of God who takes away the sins of the world. Happy are those who are called to his supper."

We respond by praying, "Lord, I am not worthy to receive you, but only say the word and I shall be healed."

Think about these words. How special is Jesus' gift of the Eucharist? How can you thank him for giving himself to you?

Now spend some time with Jesus. Imagine you are talking to him. Talk to him about what you are thinking. Listen to what he wants you to know.

Faith Summary

The Mass is the most important way Catholics pray.

Words I Learned

altar   Holy Days of Obligation

Liturgy of the Eucharist

Ways of Being Like Jesus

You are like Jesus when you give of yourself to help others.

With My Family

Give up one hour of your free time this week to help someone in your family.

 Prayer

Thank you, Jesus, for giving yourself to me. Place in my heart a great love for the Eucharist.

My Response

Write a sentence telling how you can become closer to members of your parish.

a parent page

Focus on Faith

The Eucharist, Our Home

He was a soldier overseas. On Sunday morning he went to the nearest Catholic church. The Mass was prayed in a language he did not understand, but the ritual was the same as at home. When he received Holy Communion, the soldier reflected on the parish community that had nurtured him. He realized that Jesus Christ is present in the same manner everywhere. As we go to Mass with our children we remember that we are celebrating with Catholics around the world.

Dinnertime Conversation Starter

Imagine that you and your family are attending Mass in a country where an unfamiliar language is spoken. What clues could you find in the church or in the celebration of the Mass that would indicate that it is Catholic?

Hints for at Home

Create a Jesus Sacrificed Himself for Us cross for your family. You will need poster board, scissors, photographs of your immediate and extended family, and glue. Draw a cross on the poster board and cut it out. Then invite your child to create a collage on the cross by cutting and attaching the photographs to fit. Display your completed cross in a prominent place.

Spirituality in Action

Be a role model for your child; receive Holy Communion each time you are at Mass. Help your child realize that Jesus is present with us in many ways, especially in the Eucharist. In Holy Communion we receive the Body and Blood of Jesus Christ under the appearance of bread and wine.

Focus on Prayer

Your child is learning about the Liturgy of the Eucharist in Mass. The next time you are at Mass, guide your child to be attentive during this part of the liturgy. Call to your child's attention the offertory gifts, the Lord's Prayer, and the consecration.

Review

We praise God when we attend Mass. Each Mass we celebrate brings us closer to Jesus. Celebrating the Eucharist is the most important way we live our Catholic faith.

 Prayer

Loving Jesus, be part of my life and stay with me. Keep me aware of your presence.

Faith Summary

The Sacraments of Initiation are Baptism, Confirmation, and Eucharist. Each of these sacraments gives us God's grace. In Baptism we receive the Holy Spirit, who stays with us and helps us.

Sunday is the Lord's day. We go to Mass on Sundays and on Holy Days of Obligation.

We listen to God's message during the Liturgy of the Word at Mass. The readings bring Jesus into our lives in a special way.

During the Liturgy of the Eucharist, the gifts of bread and wine become the Body and Blood of Christ. Every Mass brings Jesus into our lives.

A Poem of Our Faith

Use the words below to complete this rhyming poem.

community   Eucharist   receive

We gather for Mass, those who believe,
and new life in Jesus we will

_____ .

The Sacraments of Initiation, the Church
        does insist,
are Baptism, Confirmation, and

_____ .

We welcome Jesus with hospitality
and join with others
        in God's _____ .

Liturgy of the Eucharist

Use the words below to complete these paragraphs.

altar   Jesus   priest

bread and wine   Holy Communion

_____ shares a wonderful gift with us through the

Eucharist. During the Liturgy of the Eucharist, the gifts

are brought to the _____ .

The _____ become the Body

and Blood of Christ. This happens through the

words of consecration prayed by the _____ .

_____ is the

consecrated bread and wine we receive at Mass.

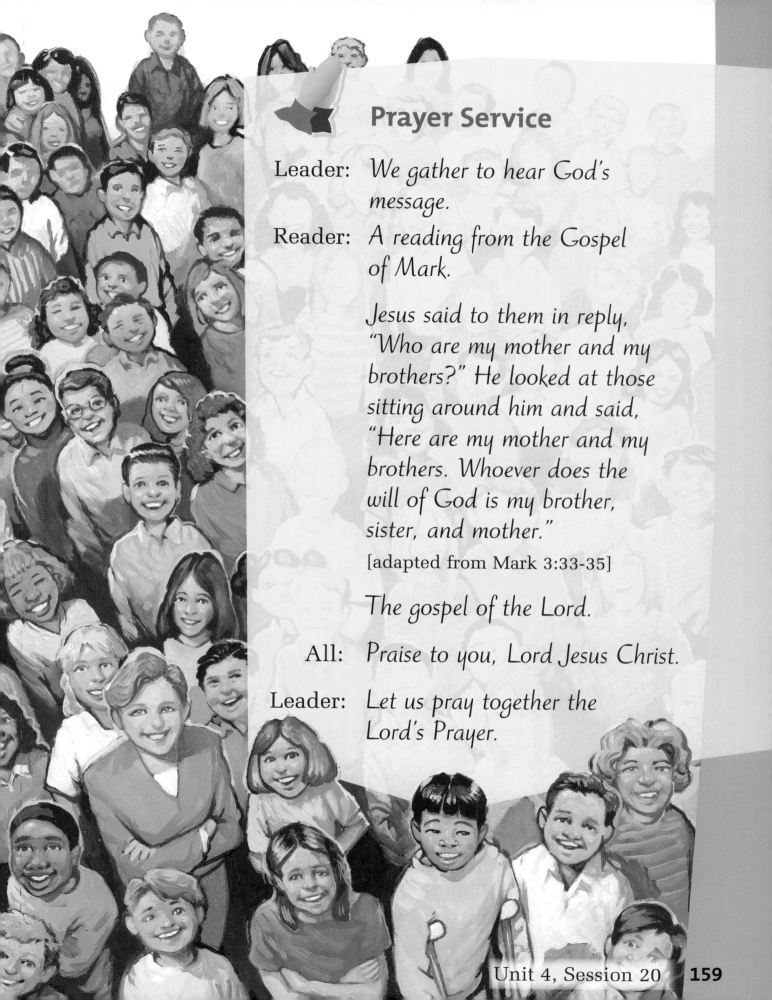

Prayer Service

Leader: We gather to hear God's message.

Reader: A reading from the Gospel of Mark.

Jesus said to them in reply, "Who are my mother and my brothers?" He looked at those sitting around him and said, "Here are my mother and my brothers. Whoever does the will of God is my brother, sister, and mother."

[adapted from Mark 3:33-35]

The gospel of the Lord.

All: Praise to you, Lord Jesus Christ.

Leader: Let us pray together the Lord's Prayer.

Living My Faith

Ways of Being Like Jesus

Jesus served God and others.
You are like Jesus when you
pray for others during Mass.

With My Family

Join your family in giving
up some of your free time
to serve members of
your community.

Prayer

*Dear Jesus, thank you for being with me as I grow
closer to you through your Church.*

My Response

Write a sentence describing a way you will
help a friend or a member of your family.

Living Like Jesus

Saint Martin of Tours

Saint Martin of Tours cared for others.
Martin's kind acts helped him find out
what God wanted him to do.

Saint Martin of Tours

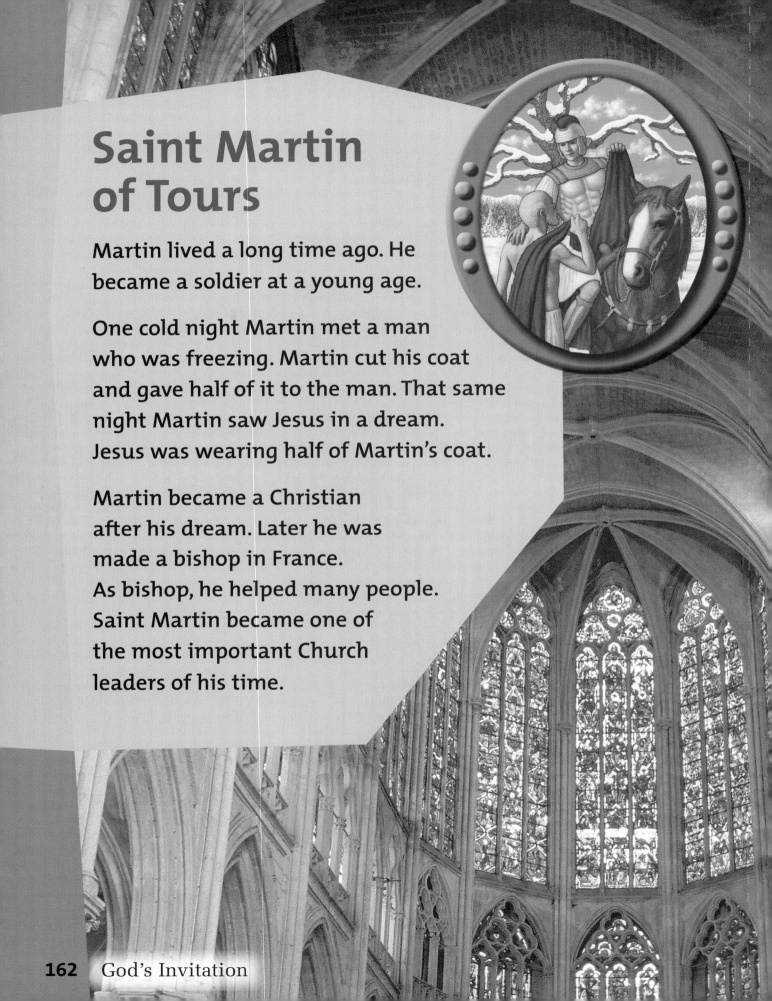

Martin lived a long time ago. He became a soldier at a young age.

One cold night Martin met a man who was freezing. Martin cut his coat and gave half of it to the man. That same night Martin saw Jesus in a dream. Jesus was wearing half of Martin's coat.

Martin became a Christian after his dream. Later he was made a bishop in France. As bishop, he helped many people. Saint Martin became one of the most important Church leaders of his time.

Being Like Jesus

Have you ever helped someone
who was sad or hurt?
How did you help this person?
How did it make you feel
about yourself?

 Prayer

*Jesus, my model of love, help me learn about the things you
said and did so I can become more like you.*

The Good Samaritan

A man asked Jesus, "What must I do to live with God forever?"

Jesus answered, "What does the law say?"

The man said, "You should love the Lord with all your strength. You should love your neighbor as much as you love yourself."

Jesus told the man that he had given the right answer. Jesus told him that he would go to heaven if he did these things.

Then the man asked Jesus, "Who is my neighbor?"

Jesus answered by telling this story. "A Jewish man was traveling on a road. He was attacked by robbers. They left him hurt in the road. A Temple official walked by and ignored the hurt man. Another man passed by and did not help him.

"Then a good man from Samaria saw him. He wanted to help. So the Good Samaritan bandaged the man's wounds, lifted him onto his donkey, and took him to an inn."

Then Jesus asked, "Which of these three men acted like a good neighbor?"

"The one who showed mercy," said the man who was questioning Jesus.

"Yes," said Jesus. "Go and be like this man."

adapted from Luke 10:25-37

Reaching Out to Others

Leyla saw Chris fall off her bike. The two girls did not always get along, but Leyla began to run toward her. Chris slowly stood up and brushed herself off.

"Are you OK?" Leyla asked.

"I think I twisted my ankle," Chris moaned.

"Take my arm," Leyla said, as she reached to help Chris. "I will help you get home. Then I will come back and get your bike for you."

"Thanks," said Chris. "I feel better already."

Reading God's Word

Blessed are people who show mercy. God will have mercy on them.

adapted from Matthew 5:7

Acting as Jesus Would

Saint Martin of Tours reached out to a suffering stranger. The Good Samaritan acted with love and mercy. Leyla helped Chris walk home. All of these people acted as Jesus would want.

Making a Difference

Check the box that shows an example of someone acting as Jesus would.

Link to Liturgy

At the end of Mass, the priest reminds us to be like Jesus. The priest says, "Go in peace to love and serve the Lord."

Prayer

Jesus asks us to show mercy in what we do and say. He wants us to act as the Good Samaritan did.

In your imagination meet Jesus in a place where you like to be. Tell Jesus you know he wants you to be kind and good to others.

Tell him about something nice that you did for someone. Then tell Jesus when it is hard for you to be nice. Ask him to help you. Listen to what Jesus will say to you.

Faith Summary

Jesus shows us how to love others through his words and actions. He wants us to help our neighbors. He wants us to care for people whom others may have forgotten.

Ways of Being Like Jesus

Be a Good Samaritan. Make a get-well card for someone who has been ill.

With My Family

Offer kind words to a family member who may be unhappy about something in his or her life.

 Prayer

Thank you, Jesus, for being my guide. Help me be a Good Samaritan for others.

My Response

Think of the people in your life who have been kind to you. Write a thank-you note to one of them.

Focus on Faith

All Are Children of God

In the musical play *South Pacific* one of the songs suggests that prejudice is something that is taught in the family. Jesus faced this issue in telling the story of the Good Samaritan. People had been taught as children not to associate with Samaritans; this group was considered unworthy. In telling the Good Samaritan story, Jesus was attacking such prejudice. Our children are absorbing our prejudices every day—in the stories we tell, in the way we interact with others in public, in the way we treat their friends. Jesus calls us to treat all people as children of God.

Dinnertime Conversation Starter

Discuss with your child ways he or she can treat others fairly. Do any prejudicial attitudes at home or school call for change?

The Good Samaritan (after Delacroix), Vincent van Gogh

In Our Parish

Organize a group of parishioners to collect blankets for a local charity or parish in need. Encourage volunteers to donate various types and sizes of blankets.

Focus on Prayer

Your child has reflected on the story of the Good Samaritan and on the ways in which he or she can show mercy to others. Share with your child a time when you extended mercy to another person. Discuss how the action made you feel. Then ask God to show you and your child ways to share his mercy.

Hints for at Home

With your child make surprise packages for the children's ward at a local hospital. You will need rolls of crepe paper, scissors, tape, ribbon, small toys, coins, pencil toppers or erasers, stickers, and other small, inexpensive treats.

Cut a 24-inch length of crepe paper. Place several items on one end of the strip and start rolling it up. Then add several more items and continue rolling in layers. Form a ball and secure its top with a ribbon. With your child deliver the completed surprise packages.

We Share God's Life

Think of a good choice you have made.
What helped you make the right choice?

 Prayer

Dear Jesus, help me to make good choices in all I do and say.

Choose Life

Moses was a great leader of the Jewish people. He led them to freedom. He reminded them of why it was important to do what God wanted.

Moses said, "Good things will happen if you obey the Ten Commandments. Love God and follow his laws. Then you will be blessed.

"You can also choose not to follow God. Then you will not be blessed. The choice is yours to make."

adapted from Deuteronomy 30:16-18

Reading God's Word

Jesus said, "I am the way, the truth, and the life."

adapted from John 14:6

Guided by God's Gifts

God has given us the Church and the Bible. These gifts teach us the difference between right and wrong. They help us make a **moral choice.**

We can get help from important people in our lives when making important choices. These people include parents, teachers, catechists, and priests. Praying to the Holy Spirit also guides us in making good choices.

Steps for Making Good Choices

Ask the Holy Spirit to help you make good choices. Then ask yourself these questions before making important decisions.

1. Is the thing I am choosing to do a good thing?

2. Am I choosing to do it for the right reasons?

3. Am I choosing to do it at the right time and in the right place?

Listening to Your Conscience

Hannah counted all the money she had. She thought, "I need more money to buy the CD I want."

Hannah would not get her allowance until Friday. But if she took money from her sister's piggy bank, she could buy the CD today.

"She will never find out," Hannah thought. Then Hannah listened to her conscience. She knew it was wrong to take what did not belong to her.

Hannah put the bank down. "I will do the right thing. I will wait until I have the money."

Link to Liturgy

At Mass we pray to Jesus, the Lamb of God, for mercy and peace.

A Good Choice

How would Hannah have felt if she had taken the money? How did she feel by not taking it? Put the words below into the correct piggy bank.

at peace   guilty   happy   nervous

Did Take

_____

_____

Did Not Take

_____

_____

Who do you think helped Hannah make the

right choice? _____ _____ _____

Did You Know?

We examine our conscience before celebrating the Sacrament of Penance. We think about times when we have not made good choices.

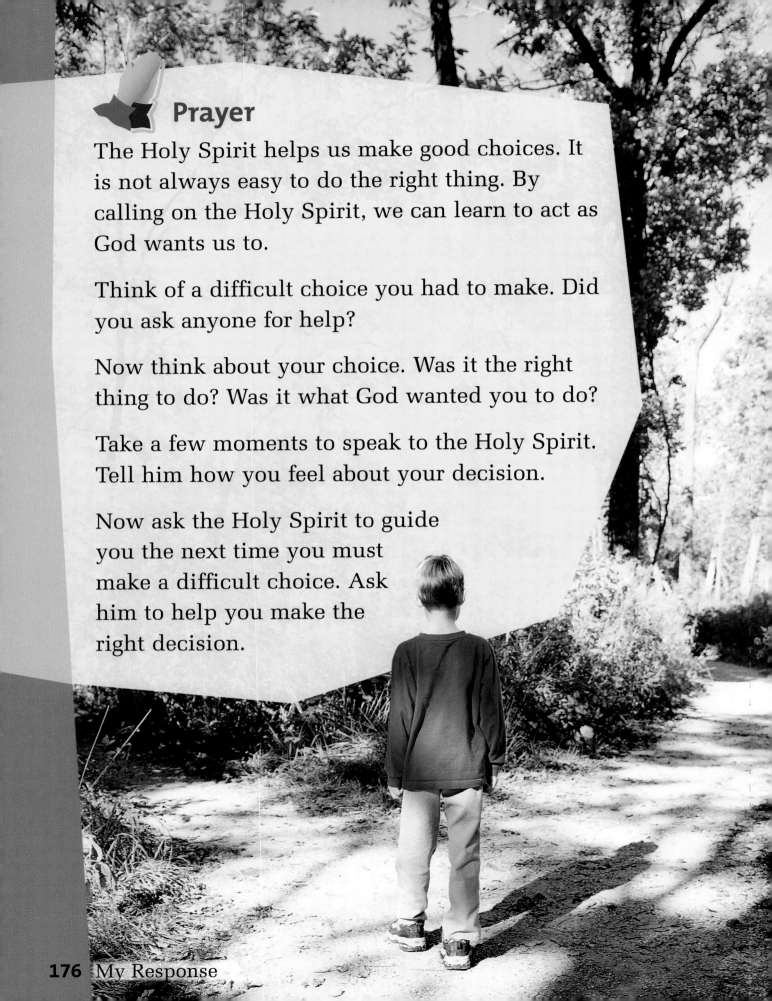

Prayer

The Holy Spirit helps us make good choices. It is not always easy to do the right thing. By calling on the Holy Spirit, we can learn to act as God wants us to.

Think of a difficult choice you had to make. Did you ask anyone for help?

Now think about your choice. Was it the right thing to do? Was it what God wanted you to do?

Take a few moments to speak to the Holy Spirit. Tell him how you feel about your decision.

Now ask the Holy Spirit to guide you the next time you must make a difficult choice. Ask him to help you make the right decision.

Faith Summary

Praying to the Holy Spirit helps us make the right choices.

Word I Learned

moral choice

Ways of Being Like Jesus

We are like Jesus when we listen to our conscience and do what God wants us to do.

With My Family

Think of an organization that has made a choice to help others. Help this organization in whatever way you can.

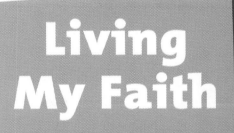

 Prayer

Thank you, God, for the people who help me.

My Response

Make a choice this week that will help another person.

a parent page

![Moses Presenting the Tablets of Law, Raphael]

Moses Presenting the Tablets of Law, Raphael

Focus on Faith

Making Choices for Life

Moses knew that he was dying and that he would never see the land God had promised. As the people prepared to cross the River Jordan, Moses delivered one final sermon. He summarized what God wanted of his people. Moses told them to choose to follow God and to obey his commandments. Our children witness our choices every day. Are the choices they see in our lives those that will lead them to choose life in God?

Dinnertime Conversation Starter

Discuss with your child the choices that he or she had to make today in school or at home. Did these decisions affect his or her relationship with God? Help your child develop a method for making good decisions.

Hints for at Home

With your child make a Do the Right Thing display in your home. Trace and cut out doves, using this Holy Spirit pattern. Each time a member of your family makes a good choice, write the person's name on one of the doves. Post the display in a prominent location and watch it grow as your child becomes more aware of the ways in which to do the right thing!

Spirituality in Action

Act as a moral barometer for your child. Discuss with him or her daily occurrences that require moral choices to be made. Guide your child to do the right thing through discussion of the issue at hand, its possible outcomes, the way you and God would want your child to act, and the circumstances and repercussions of the choice. Acknowledge and affirm your child's decision when he or she makes a good choice.

Focus on Prayer

Your child has reflected about the ways in which the Holy Spirit assists him or her in making good choices. With your child offer a prayer of thanksgiving to the Holy Spirit.

Following Jesus

Think of a time when someone was kind to you. What did you think of this person? How did this person's actions make you want to treat others?

 Prayer

Jesus, help me to treat others with love and kindness as you do.

The Great Commandment

The **Old Testament** is the story of God's love for the Jewish people. The **New Testament** is the story of Jesus' life. It also tells how the early Church lived like Jesus.

In the New Testament Jesus gave us the **Great Commandment.** It teaches us how to follow God and care for others. Thinking about the Great Commandment helps us make moral choices. We make the right choice when we love God and others.

Reading God's Word

Love God with all your heart, soul, and mind. Love your neighbor as yourself. This is the greatest commandment.

adapted from Matthew 22:37-38

The Beatitudes

Jesus wanted us to be happy. So he taught us the **Beatitudes.**

Jesus said, "Blessed are those who are kind to others. They will be rewarded.

"Blessed are those who do the right thing even when it is difficult. They will be with God one day.

"Blessed are those who are fair to others. They will be treated fairly.

"Blessed are those who work for peace. They are God's children."

adapted from Matthew 5:1-10

When Jesus gave us the Beatitudes, he taught us how to be happy with one another.

Love Your Neighbor

Tina noticed her neighbor, Amanda, looking out the window. Amanda looked sad.

Tina went home and told her mom that Amanda looked sad. Tina wondered what she could do for Amanda.

"Tina," her mom said, smiling, "you are doing what Jesus teaches when you care for your neighbor. Invite Amanda to come over and play."

Doing What Jesus Teaches

In the stories below, Nadia, Jerome, and Arturo each have to make a difficult choice. Below each story, write the good choice each person can make to follow the Beatitudes.

1. Will forgets to bring his crayons to art class. Nadia just got new crayons, and she does not want anyone to ruin them.

_____

2. Jerome is helping his sister with an assignment. He really wants to go outside to play.

_____

3. Two children get into a fight on the playground. Arturo and all the other children stop and watch.

_____

Meet a Saint

Elizabeth Ann Seton always found time to help others. She started the first Catholic grade school in the United States. Elizabeth was the first American-born person to be named a saint.

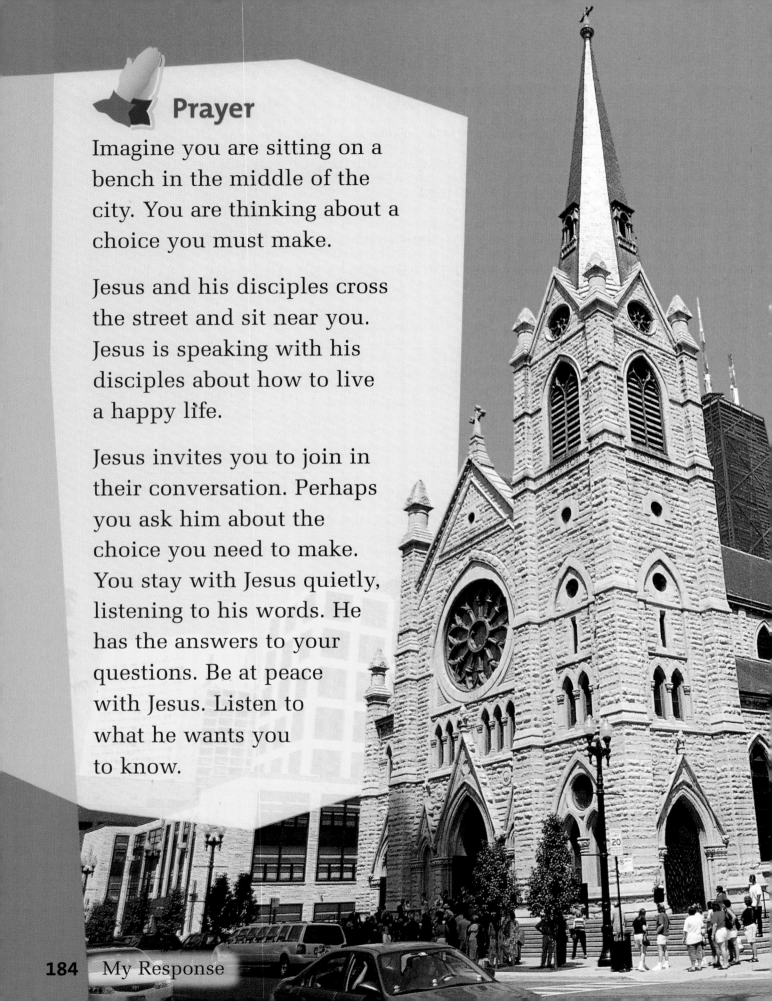

Prayer

Imagine you are sitting on a bench in the middle of the city. You are thinking about a choice you must make.

Jesus and his disciples cross the street and sit near you. Jesus is speaking with his disciples about how to live a happy life.

Jesus invites you to join in their conversation. Perhaps you ask him about the choice you need to make. You stay with Jesus quietly, listening to his words. He has the answers to your questions. Be at peace with Jesus. Listen to what he wants you to know.

Faith Summary

In the Great Commandment Jesus told us to love God and others. Jesus gave us the Beatitudes to help us live a happy life.

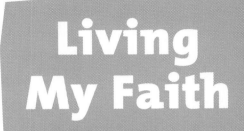

Words I Learned

Beatitudes   Great Commandment

New Testament   Old Testament

Ways of Being Like Jesus

Treat others with respect in everything you do this week.

With My Family

Comfort a family member or neighbor who is ill or unhappy.

 Prayer

Thank you, Jesus, for the Beatitudes. Thank you for your help in trying to live them every day.

My Response

Choose a beatitude to practice this week.

Focus on Faith

Loving as God Loves

When Blessed Mother Teresa was laboring for the poor, a reporter asked her what she thought about being called a saint. She replied that we are all called to be saints. She was called to be a saint in what she did, and the reporters, cameramen, and producers were called to be saints in what they did. This is the biblical understanding of what it means to be holy. A holy person is someone who responds to God's call to love him and serve others. As parents we also are called to be holy. We respond to God's call by serving our family members and by showing them God's love.

Dinnertime Conversation Starter

Recall with your family memorable people who have touched your lives. What made them special? How did they serve God and others?

Hints for at Home

With your child create Happy Hand Towels for a homeless shelter. You will need new hand towels and a black permanent marker. Invite your child to draw a smiley face on each towel; ask him or her to write an upbeat message, such as *Jesus loves you* or *Blessed are the clean of heart* on each. With your family deliver the completed towels.

Focus on Prayer

Your child has learned the importance of praying for help in making good choices. With your child take a few moments to offer a prayer for help when making difficult choices.

Spirituality in Action

Go with your child to visit a sick or elderly relative, neighbor, or parishioner. Bring along a snack, holy cards, magazines, and a board game. Spend some time visiting, talking, and playing the game with the elderly friend. Afterwards ask your child to share how he or she felt during the visit. Reinforce the idea that when we reach out to those in need, we are loving our neighbors.

Making Choices

Think of a time when someone played with your toys. Did this person respect you and your belongings? How can you respect others?

Prayer

Jesus, you want me to live in peace with others.
Show me how to be a peacemaker.

A Community of Believers

Peter wanted to teach the Christians about God's plan for them. So he wrote a letter.

Peter wrote, "Whoever loves their life should not tell lies or say evil things. Do what is right and stay away from evil. Bring peace into the world."

adapted from 1 Peter 3:10-12

Reading God's Word

If you want to be happy, do not say bad things or tell lies. Always be peaceful with one another, and do not sin.

adapted from Psalm 34:12-15

Respect Others

Ana and Eduardo said hurtful things about Benito. They did not know that Benito could hear them. Later they wished that they had not said mean things about him.

Harmful words hurt everyone. Benito was hurt by what Ana and Eduardo said. Ana and Eduardo felt ashamed for talking about Benito. They knew that they should never say hurtful things about others.

Like Ana and Eduardo, we can be tempted to say hurtful things about others. But God wants us to treat everybody with kindness. He teaches us that we will be happy if we show respect for others and their feelings.

Showing Respect

Write **R** on the line if the person is being respectful. Write **NR** if the person is not being respectful.

1. Tucker makes fun of Corey's haircut. _____

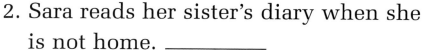

2. Sara reads her sister's diary when she is not home. _____

3. Kevin thanks Holly for helping him. _____

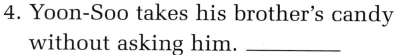

4. Yoon-Soo takes his brother's candy without asking him. _____

5. Maria cleans her sister's bike after borrowing it. _____

 **Link to Liturgy**

The sign of peace at Mass is one way we show respect for others.

Living in Kindness

God wants us to live in kindness. He wants us to be kind to one another and to enjoy the kindness others show us.

When we steal, lie, or say unkind things about others, we sin. God wants us to make up for what we have done. We ask for forgiveness. We return what was stolen. We stop saying hurtful things. Then we can live in kindness as God wants us to.

 Meet a Saint

Saint Francis Borgia was a rich man. One day, Francis gave away his money and became a priest. He helped others and served the Church for the rest of his life.

Prayer

Imagine you are sitting quietly by yourself. As you are sitting there, Jesus walks up to you.

You begin talking to Jesus about how you have grown closer to him this year. Maybe you talk about the happy and sad times you have had. Know that you can share whatever you want to with Jesus.

You can ask him for whatever you need.

Spend some quiet time listening to Jesus. Talk to him from your heart. Listen to what he wants you to know.

Faith Summary

Jesus teaches us to respect people and their belongings. We will be happy if we are respectful in our words and actions.

Ways of Being Like Jesus

Jesus was kind to everyone. You are like Jesus when you are kind to others.

With My Family

Discuss with your family what you can do to live peacefully together.

Prayer

Thank you, Jesus, for all you have taught me. Help me to respect everyone in my life.

My Response

Write a way you can show respect for the belongings of others.

Focus on Faith

Our Priorities

Francis Borgia (1510–1572) was a rich nobleman in Spain. He enjoyed being a person of wealth and high social standing. Then one day a close friend died, and Francis realized that his wealth would not last forever or buy him happiness. After his wife died, Francis became a Jesuit priest and was eventually made the head of the order. No longer focused on money and material possessions, Francis had shifted his attention toward serving God. Like Francis, we make decisions every day that teach our children where our priorities lie. They can see how important God is in our lives. If they made a list of what is important to them, where would God rank?

Dinnertime Conversation Starter

Talk about the importance of God in your family life. What are the ways you show that God is a priority in your home?

The Vision of St. Francis Borgia, with Sts. Aloysius Gonzaga and Stanislaus Kostka, Antonio Salas

Hints for at Home

With your family create a Respect poster. You will need watercolor paint, a tin pan, poster board, and a permanent marker. Place the paint in the tin pan and allow each member of your family to take a turn placing his or her hand in the paint. Have each family member place a handprint on the poster board. When each hand is in place, write *Respect* on the poster with the permanent marker. Place the completed poster in a prominent place in your home to remind your family to respect one another's property, good name, and privacy.

Spirituality in Action

With your family make a pledge of peace. Such a pledge encourages respect and forgiveness and opposes the use of violence. With your family join hands in a circle of peace. Recite the pledge "We pledge to respect one another, to listen to one another, and to forgive one another. We pledge to respect all of God's creation. We pledge to oppose violence in all forms and to live our lives in peace."

Focus on Prayer

Your child has learned that the sign of peace is one way we show our care and respect for others. Notice the sign of peace the next time you are at Mass with your child. Discuss the ways in which it strengthens our ties as parishioners and community members.

Review

Jesus is our friend, our Savior, and our model of love and goodness. He is our greatest gift from God.

 Prayer

Jesus, you are my light and my life. May your love help me continue to grow to be more like you.

Faith Summary

Jesus shows us how to love others through his words and actions. He gave us an example in the parable of the Good Samaritan.

The Holy Spirit helps us to make moral choices in our lives.

Jesus taught us the Great Commandment and the Beatitudes. They will help us bring peace into our lives and the lives of others.

Jesus wants us to be kind to others. He asks us to respect others and their belongings.

Living Like Jesus

Complete the sentences.
The answers are found in the box.

choices	Commandment	mercy
peace	Samaritan	Testament

1. We make good moral _____ when we ask for God's help.

2. The New _____ tells the story of Jesus' life.

3. The Good _____ did as Jesus teaches.

4. The Great _____ tells us how to love God and others.

5. Showing _____ is one way to be like Jesus.

6. Jesus said, "Blessed are those who work for _____."

Prayer for Peace

In the heart write a peace prayer for the prayer service.

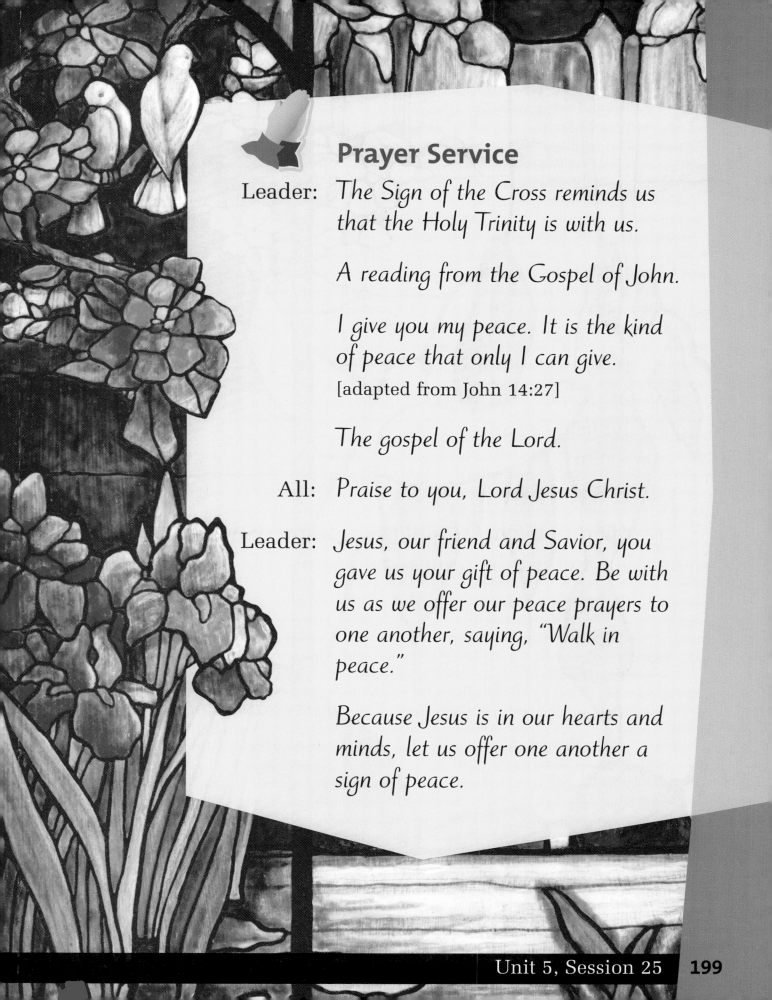

Prayer Service

Leader: The Sign of the Cross reminds us that the Holy Trinity is with us.

A reading from the Gospel of John.

I give you my peace. It is the kind of peace that only I can give.
[adapted from John 14:27]

The gospel of the Lord.

All: Praise to you, Lord Jesus Christ.

Leader: Jesus, our friend and Savior, you gave us your gift of peace. Be with us as we offer our peace prayers to one another, saying, "Walk in peace."

Because Jesus is in our hearts and minds, let us offer one another a sign of peace.

Living My Faith

Ways of Being Like Jesus

Jesus gave the world the gift of peace. You are like Jesus when you live in peace with your family, friends, and others.

With My Family

Treat family members and their property with respect. Return the things you borrow.

Prayer

Peaceful Jesus, thank you for all you have done for me. Help me make the right choices in everything I do and say.

My Response

What can you do to bring peace to others?

The Year in Our Church

Ordinary Time
Christmas
Lent
Holy Week

Epiphany
Ash Wednesday
Palm Sunday
Holy Thursday
Good Friday
Holy Saturday
Easter Sunday

Christmas

Advent

Easter

First Sunday of Advent

All Souls Day
All Saints Day

Ascension
Pentecost

Winter Spring
Fall Summer

Ordinary Time

Liturgical Calendar
The liturgical calendar shows us the feasts and seasons of the Church year.

Liturgical Year

We get our hearts ready to welcome Jesus during **Advent.**

Christmas celebrates Jesus' birth. **Epiphany** celebrates Jesus' coming for all people of the world.

Lent prepares us for Easter. It is a time to do extra good deeds.

During **Holy Week** we remember the suffering and death of Jesus.

On **Easter** we recall with joy Jesus' rising from the dead.

Pentecost is the feast of the Holy Spirit's coming to guide the Church.

All Saints Day celebrates all the holy persons who died and now live with God in heaven.

Ordinary Time is time set aside for everyday living as followers of Jesus.

Advent

We get ready to celebrate Jesus' birth in Advent.
A long time ago Saint John the Baptist helped
people get ready for Jesus.

Prayer

Dear God, help me this Advent to pray and to share.

Preparing for Jesus' Birth

Sometimes it is hard to wait. When we have a birthday party, we get ready. Then we wait and wait. We are excited. We celebrate when our birthday guests arrive.

During Advent we get ready to celebrate the birth of Jesus. Advent is our time of waiting.

Waiting for Jesus

People asked John the Baptist how to get ready for Jesus. John told the people to share and to help one another. He told them to be honest. He told them not to steal from one another.

adapted from Luke 3:10-14

The Advent Wreath

The Advent wreath has four candles. There is one candle for each of the four weeks of Advent. During these four weeks we prepare to celebrate Jesus' birth. We pray and do good deeds for others. This is what John the Baptist told the people to do.

Welcoming Jesus

Draw a picture to put in your home that shows how you are preparing for Jesus' birth.

Prayer Service

Leader: *John the Baptist helped people change their lives. He helped them get ready for Jesus. Let us pray this Advent that we will be ready to follow Jesus.*

A reading from the Book of Psalms.

I wait for you, O Lord. Teach me to follow your path. Guide me in your truth, because you are God, my Savior. I will wait for you all day.

[adapted from Psalm 25:4–5]

All: *Jesus is the light of the world. The world is brighter when we are a light for others.*

Christmas and Epiphany

Three wise men traveled far to find Jesus.
They wanted to honor him.

 Prayer

*Jesus, my Savior, help me to be a gift to others as you
are to me.*

The Three Wise Men

The wise men were looking for the new king. They wanted to worship him. They saw his star.

The star led the wise men to Bethlehem. There they saw Jesus with Mary and Joseph. They gave Jesus gifts of gold, frankincense, and myrrh.

The wise men then returned home.

adapted from Matthew 2:1-12

The Wise Men's Gifts

Gold, frankincense, and myrrh were very special gifts. The wise men gave these gifts to Jesus because they knew he was special. We can be like the wise men by making Jesus special in our lives too.

Jesus, Our Gift

Jesus is God's gift to us. He teaches us how to be gifts to others. We can do this by bringing Jesus' love into the world.

We can respect those who are not popular or rich. We can be friends to children who do not have many friends. We can care for someone who is ill. When we do these things, we are being gifts to others.

Give a Special Gift

Fill out the gift tag. Then on the lines below tell about a gift of yourself that you will give someone this Christmas.

To:

From:

_____

_____

_____

_____

Prayer Service

Leader: God gave us the greatest Christmas gift, his Son. Let us rejoice and adore Jesus, our Savior.

Reader: A reading from the Gospel of Matthew.

Bethlehem is a small town, but it is very important. A ruler will come from this town.
[adapted from Matthew 2:6]

The gospel of the Lord.

All: Praise to you, Lord Jesus Christ.

Leader: Jesus, God's Son, is born for us.

All: Come, let us adore him.

Lent

Jesus loves little children.
He tells his disciples to
be like children.

 Prayer

Jesus, my friend, teach me this Lent how to live as a child of God. I want to love God as you do.

Depending on Jesus

The disciples asked Jesus, "Who is the greatest in the kingdom of heaven?" Jesus called a child to come join them.

He said, "You must become like this child. Then you will live with God in heaven."

adapted from Matthew 18:1-4

We Depend on God

Parents reach out to help their children. Children depend on their parents. We are all God's children. God reaches out to us. We need his help.

Making Changes

Jesus asked his disciples to change. Lent is a time for change. We ask ourselves questions: How can I help others? How can I stay close to God? How can I be more like Jesus?

We receive ashes on our forehead on Ash Wednesday. This is when we tell God how we will change our lives. These ashes remind us that we should follow Jesus.

Changing for the Better

What could you do to make the bad situations good? Draw a line to connect each box on the top row with its matching box on the bottom row.

Prayer Service

Leader: Let us begin our prayer with the Sign of the Cross.

Jesus taught us how to pray to God our Father. Let us tell Jesus that we will listen to him and follow him.

Reader: A reading from the Book of Psalms.

God loves those who hate evil. He protects those who are faithful. He rescues them from the wicked. If you are fair and honest, God will be with you.

[adapted from Psalm 97:10–11]

Leader: Let us close by praying the Lord's Prayer together.

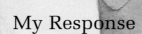

Holy Week

Jesus was kind and loving to everyone. Jesus prayed for his enemies. How can you be like Jesus during Holy Week?

 Prayer

*Jesus, my helper, help me forgive those who hurt me.
I want to love others as you did.*

Jesus' Great Love

Jesus was talking to his friends when a crowd arrived. A judge and his servant were part of the crowd. They came to arrest Jesus.

Jesus' friends rushed to help him. One of them cut the ear of the judge's servant. Jesus told his friend to stop. Jesus touched the servant's ear, and it was healed.

adapted from Luke 22:47-51

The Touch of Love

Jesus knew he would be arrested. Still, he reached out to his enemies with a healing touch. Jesus did not try to get even. He showed love instead.

We are called to be like Jesus. We are not to harm those who do not like us. We can show love by praying for them and by being kind.

Acts of Love

Write acts of love you will do during Holy Week to be like Jesus.

Prayer Service

Leader: Jesus was a loving person even when he was about to be arrested. Let us listen to what Jesus tells us about loving others.

Reader: A reading from the Gospel of Matthew.

You have heard people say, "You shall love your friend and hate your enemy." But I say that you should love your enemy. You should pray for those who hurt you. Then you will be children of God.

[adapted from Matthew 5:43–45]

The gospel of the Lord.

All: Praise to you, Lord Jesus Christ.

Leader: Let us remember that Jesus wants us to show his love as we pray the Sign of the Cross.

Easter

Easter is a joyful time. We celebrate that Jesus is risen.

 Prayer

Dear Jesus, help me be a person of joy. I want to help others be joyful too.

Looking for Jesus

Mary Magdalene and other women went to Jesus' tomb. They brought spices to put on his body. When they got there, the tomb was empty. An angel was there. The angel said to them, "Go and tell the disciples that Jesus is risen. He will meet them."

adapted from Mark 16:1-7

Meeting Jesus in Others

The women at the tomb were followers of Jesus. The angel's message meant that the disciples would meet Jesus in the people they would serve.

We meet Jesus in our lives when we help others. Who are the people we can love and serve?

Sunday, the Lord's Day

On this day we remember that Jesus rose from the dead. We celebrate the Resurrection on Sunday, the Lord's day.

Loving and Serving Others

Write ways you love and serve others. These are ways you meet Jesus in your life.

_____

_____

_____

Prayer Service

Leader: *We meet Jesus in those we love and serve. We meet Jesus in a special way at Mass. Let us rejoice that the Lord is with us.*

A reading from the Book of Psalms.

Group A: *Sing to the Lord a new song.*

Group B: *Sing to the Lord, all the earth.*

Group A: *Sing to the Lord and praise his name.*

Group B: *Sing day after day.*

All: *The Lord has saved us!*
[adapted from Psalm 96:1–2]

Leader: *Let us continue to praise Jesus by loving one another.*

All: *Amen. Alleluia.*

Pentecost

The coming of the Holy Spirit is celebrated on Pentecost. The Holy Spirit came to Peter and the other disciples. They told everyone about Jesus.

 Prayer

Jesus, teach me how to help others the way the disciples did.

Peter Helps

With the other disciples Peter received the Holy Spirit on Pentecost. He wanted to tell people about Jesus.

Peter was going to the Temple to pray. He saw a poor man who could not walk. The man begged for money. Peter said, "I do not have silver or gold. What I do have, I will give you. In the name of Jesus Christ, get up and walk."

The man leaped up and walked around. He was very excited. He went into the Temple and praised God.

adapted from Acts of the Apostles 3:1-8

How did Peter's actions change the man's life?

What Can You Do?

Like Peter, you have the help of the Holy Spirit. The Spirit leads you to pray and to care for others. Below each situation write what you could do to help the person in need.

1. Justin was absent from school. He needs help with his homework to catch up to the rest of his class.

_____

2. Little Sara is crying. No one will help her learn how to ride her new bike.

_____

3. Mona is feeling sad because the children at her new school do not include her.

_____

4. Jimmy wants to be on the soccer team, but he does not know how to play.

_____

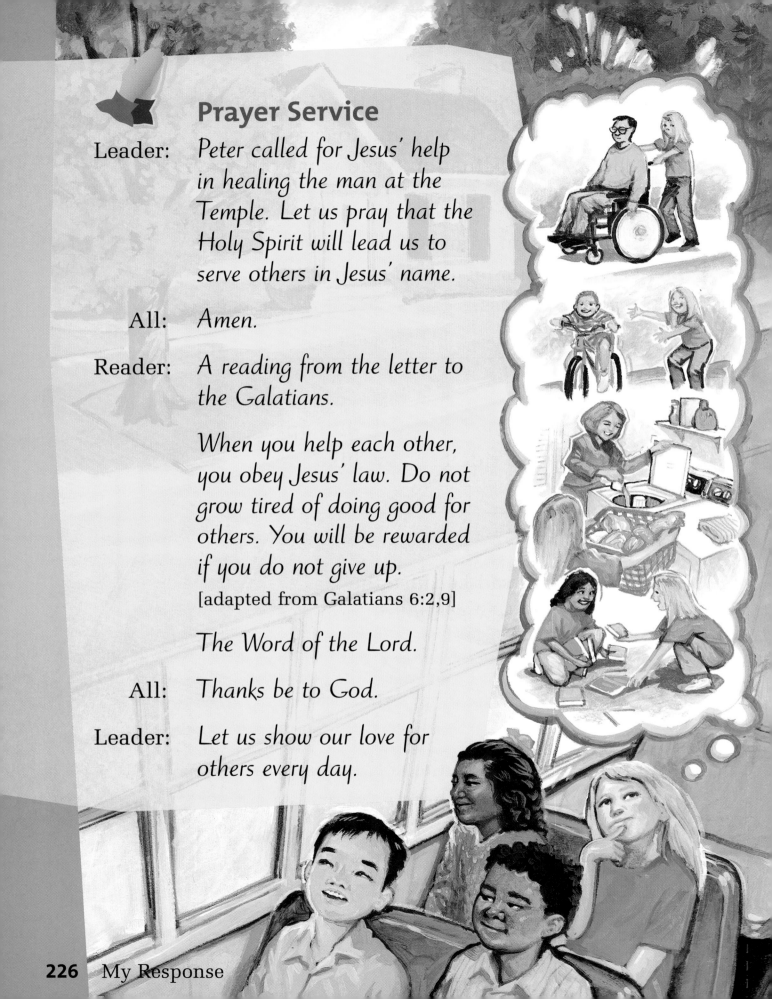

Prayer Service

Leader: Peter called for Jesus' help in healing the man at the Temple. Let us pray that the Holy Spirit will lead us to serve others in Jesus' name.

All: Amen.

Reader: A reading from the letter to the Galatians.

When you help each other, you obey Jesus' law. Do not grow tired of doing good for others. You will be rewarded if you do not give up.
[adapted from Galatians 6:2,9]

The Word of the Lord.

All: Thanks be to God.

Leader: Let us show our love for others every day.

All Saints Day

On the Feast of All Saints we remember the saints in heaven. We want to become saints too. We want to live as children of God.

 ## Prayer

Jesus, my brother, I want to follow you and be close to you.

Becoming Children of God

The people wanted to become children of God. So they asked Peter and Jesus' other disciples what they should do.

Peter said, "Be sorry for your sins and be baptized in the name of Jesus Christ. Your sins will be forgiven. You will receive the gift of the Holy Spirit. This promise is made for everyone God calls."

adapted from Acts of the Apostles 2:37-39

Living as God's Children

Jesus wants us to be close to him and to one another. He gives us the grace of the sacraments to help us. He asks us to pray for one another and for those who died. We ask the saints in heaven to pray for us. We are all together in Jesus. This is the Communion of Saints.

Feast of All Saints

On November 1 we celebrate the Feast of All Saints. We go to Mass. We remember those who have died and now live with God.

It is also a good time to think about the special people in your life. Think of how they help you. Think of their good example. Think of their love for you.

In the frame draw a picture of one special person in your life. Write a sentence to tell why this person is special to you.

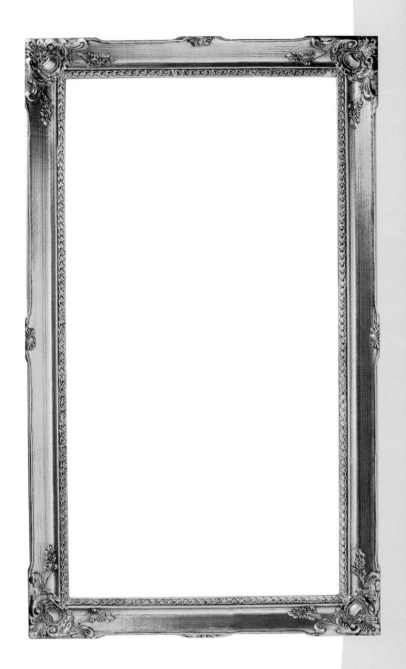

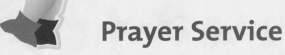

Prayer Service

Leader: *Jesus asks us to pray for one another.*

We pray for those who have died. Lord, have mercy on them.

All: *Lord, have mercy on them.*

Leader: *We ask the saints in heaven to pray for us. Holy saints, help us to follow Jesus.*

All: *Holy saints, help us to follow Jesus.*

Reader: *A reading from the first letter of John.*

Beloved, we are God's children now.
[1 John 3:2]

The Word of the Lord.

All: *Thanks be to God.*

Leader: *Let us close with the prayer to God the Father that Jesus taught us.*

Prayers and Practices of Our Faith

Grade 2

CELEBRATING OUR FAITH

LIVING OUR FAITH

SONGS OF OUR FAITH

UNDERSTANDING THE WORDS OF OUR FAITH

The Bible and You

God speaks to us in many ways. One way is through the Bible. The Bible is the story of God's promise to care for us, especially through his Son, Jesus.

The Bible is made up of two parts. The Old Testament tells stories about the Jewish people before Jesus was born.

In the New Testament Jesus teaches us about the Father's love. The Gospels tell stories about Jesus' life, death, and resurrection.

At Mass we hear stories from the Bible. We can also read the Bible on our own.

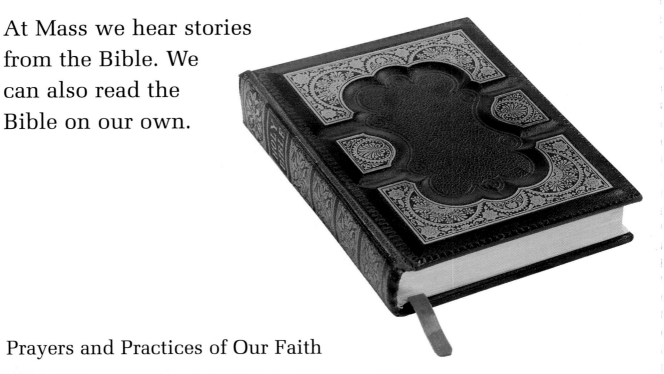

Prayer and How We Pray

Prayer is talking and listening to God. We can talk to God in the words of special prayers or in our own words. We can pray aloud or quietly in our hearts.

We can pray to God often and in many different ways. We praise God. We can ask God for what we need and thank him. We can pray for ourselves and for others.

Prayers to Take to Heart

It is good for us to know prayers by heart. To learn prayers by heart means that we not only learn, or memorize, the words but try to understand and live them.

Glory Be to the Father

Glory be to the Father,
and to the Son,
and to the Holy Spirit.
As it was in the beginning,
is now, and ever shall be,
world without end.
Amen.

Sign of the Cross

In the name of the Father,
and of the Son,
and of the Holy Spirit.
Amen.

In the name of the Father,   *and of the Son,*

and of the Holy   *Spirit.*   *Amen.*

Lord's Prayer

Our Father,
who art in heaven,
hallowed be thy name;
thy kingdom come;
thy will be done
on earth as it is in heaven.
Give us this day our daily bread;
and forgive us our trespasses
as we forgive those
who trespass against us;
and lead us not into temptation,
but deliver us from evil.
Amen.

Knowing and Praying Our Faith **237**

Hail Mary

Hail Mary, full of grace,
the Lord is with you.
Blessed are you among women,
and blessed is the fruit of your womb, Jesus.
Holy Mary, Mother of God,
pray for us sinners,
now and at the hour of our death.
Amen.

Act of Contrition

My God,
I am sorry for my sins with all my heart.
In choosing to do wrong
and failing to do good,
I have sinned against you
whom I should love above all things.
I firmly intend, with your help,
to do penance,
to sin no more,
and to avoid whatever leads me to sin.
Our Savior Jesus Christ
suffered and died for us.
In his name, my God, have mercy.

Prayer to the Holy Spirit

Come, Holy Spirit,
fill the hearts of your faithful.
And kindle in them
the fire of your love.
Send forth your Spirit
and they shall be created.
And you will renew
the face of the earth.

Morning Prayer

God, our Father, I offer you today
all that I think and do and say.
I offer it with what was done
on earth by Jesus Christ, your Son.
Amen.

Evening Prayer

God, our Father, this day is done.
We ask you and Jesus Christ, your Son,
that with the Spirit, our welcome guest,
you guard our sleep and bless our rest.
Amen.

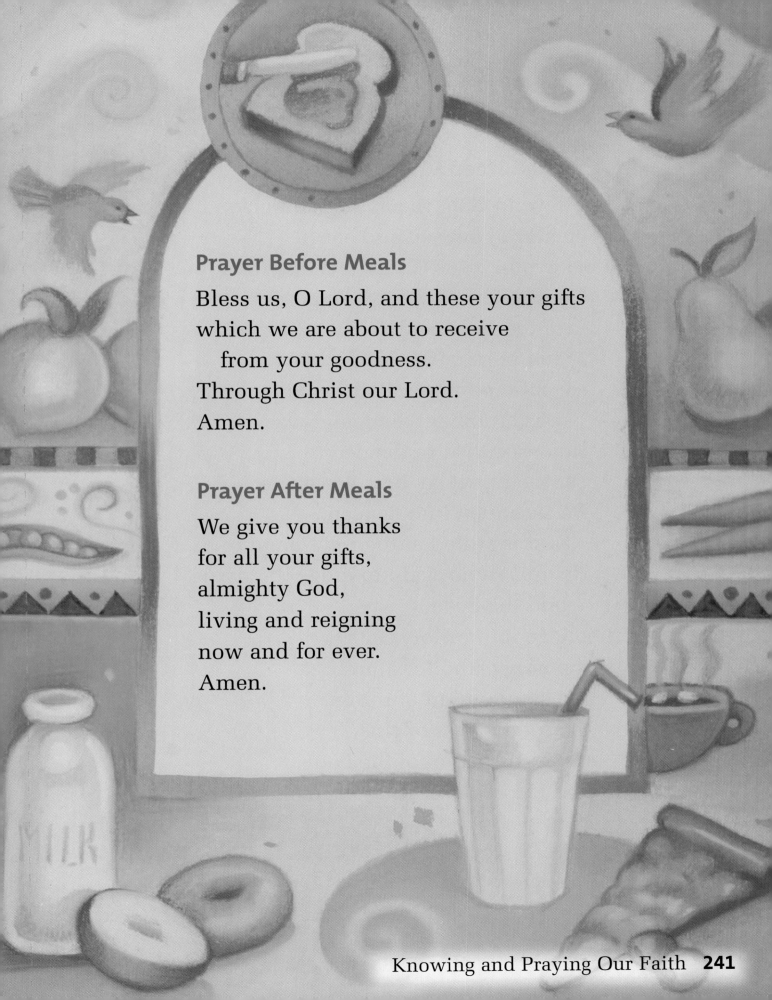

Prayer Before Meals

Bless us, O Lord, and these your gifts
which we are about to receive
  from your goodness.
Through Christ our Lord.
Amen.

Prayer After Meals

We give you thanks
for all your gifts,
almighty God,
living and reigning
now and for ever.
Amen.

Apostles' Creed

I believe in God, the Father almighty,
  creator of heaven and earth.
I believe in Jesus Christ, his only Son, our Lord.
  He was conceived by the power
    of the Holy Spirit
    and born of the Virgin Mary.
  He suffered under Pontius Pilate,
    was crucified, died, and was buried.
  He descended to the dead.
  On the third day he arose again.
  He ascended into heaven,
    and is seated at the right hand of the Father.
  He will come again to judge the living
    and the dead.
I believe in the Holy Spirit,
  the holy catholic Church,
  the communion of saints,
  the forgiveness of sins,
  the resurrection of the body,
  and the life everlasting. Amen.

Hail, Holy Queen

Hail, holy Queen, Mother of mercy,
hail, our life, our sweetness, and our hope.
To you we cry, the children of Eve;
to you we send up our sighs,
mourning and weeping in this
   land of exile.
Turn, then, most gracious advocate,
your eyes of mercy toward us;
lead us home at last
and show us the blessed
   fruit of your womb, Jesus:
O clement, O loving,
   O sweet Virgin Mary.

Prayer for Vocations

God, thank you for loving me.
You have called me
to live as your child.
Help all your children
to love you and one another.
Amen.

The Rosary

The Rosary helps us to reflect on the special events, or mysteries, in the lives of Jesus and Mary.

We begin by praying the Sign of the Cross while holding the crucifix. Then we pray the Apostles' Creed.

We pray the Lord's Prayer as we hold the first single bead. On each of the next three beads, we pray a Hail Mary. Next, we pray a Glory Be to the Father. On the next single bead we think about the first mystery, a particular event in the lives of Jesus and Mary. We then pray the Lord's Prayer.

The five sets of ten beads are called decades. As we pray each decade, we reflect on a different mystery. Between the sets is a single bead on which we think about one of the mysteries and pray the Lord's Prayer. We then pray a Hail Mary as we hold each of the beads in the set. At the end of each set, we pray the Glory Be to the Father.

We end by praying the Sign of the Cross while holding the crucifix.

Praying the Rosary

10. Think about the fourth mystery. Pray the Lord's Prayer.

9. Pray ten Hail Marys and one Glory Be to the Father.

11. Pray ten Hail Marys and one Glory Be to the Father.

8. Think about the third mystery. Pray the Lord's Prayer.

12. Think about the fifth mystery. Pray the Lord's Prayer.

7. Pray ten Hail Marys and one Glory Be to the Father.

6. Think about the second mystery. Pray the Lord's Prayer.

5. Pray ten Hail Marys and one Glory Be to the Father.

4. Think about the first mystery. Pray the Lord's Prayer.

3. Pray three Hail Marys and one Glory Be to the Father.

13. Pray ten Hail Marys and one Glory Be to the Father.

2. Pray the Lord's Prayer.

14. Pray the Sign of the Cross.

1. Pray the Sign of the Cross and the Apostles' Creed.

The Seven Sacraments

The sacraments are signs of the grace we receive from God.

Sacraments show that God is part of our lives. They were given to the Church by Jesus to show that he loves us. The seven sacraments help us to live the way God wants us to live. The sacraments are celebrated with us by priests.

Baptism

Baptism is the first sacrament we receive. Through Baptism we become followers of Jesus and part of God's family, the Church.

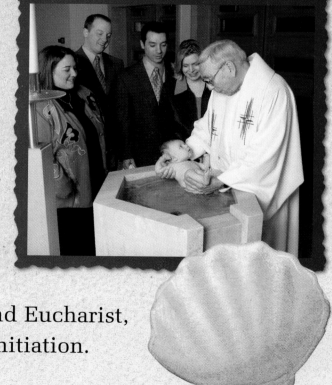

The pouring of water is the main sign of Baptism. Along with Confirmation and Eucharist, Baptism is a Sacrament of Initiation.

Confirmation

Confirmation is a Sacrament of Initiation.

In this sacrament the Holy Spirit strengthens us to be witnesses to Jesus. Confirmation makes us stronger in faith and helps us become better Christians.

The bishop places holy oil on our foreheads in the form of a cross. This is the main sign of Confirmation.

Eucharist

Eucharist is a Sacrament of Initiation.

At Mass the bread and wine become Jesus' Body and Blood. This happens when the priest says the words of consecration that Jesus used at the Last Supper. Eucharist is also called Holy Communion.

Penance

We ask God to forgive our sins in the Sacrament of Penance. The priest who celebrates this sacrament with us shares Jesus' gifts of peace and forgiveness.

God always forgives us when we are sorry and do penance for our sins.

Anointing of the Sick

In this sacrament a sick person is anointed with holy oil and receives the spiritual—and sometimes even physical—healing of Jesus.

priest   **deacon**   **bishop**

Holy Orders

Some men are called to be deacons, priests, or bishops. They receive the Sacrament of Holy Orders. Through Holy Orders the mission, or task, given by Jesus to his apostles continues in the Church.

Matrimony

Some men and women are called to be married. In the Sacrament of Matrimony, they make a solemn promise to be partners for life, both for their own good and for the good of the children they will raise.

Celebrating Our Faith   **249**

Celebrating the Lord's Day

Sunday is the day on which we celebrate the Resurrection of Jesus. Sunday is the Lord's day. We gather for Mass and rest from work. People all over the world gather at God's eucharistic table as brothers and sisters.

Order of the Mass

The Mass is the high point of the Christian life, and it always follows a set order.

Introductory Rite
preparing to celebrate the Eucharist

Entrance Procession and Song

We gather as a community and praise God in song.

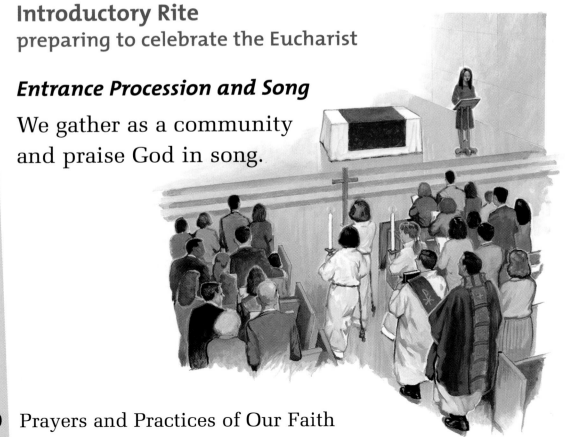

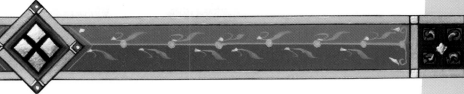

Sign of the Cross and Greeting

We pray the Sign of the Cross. The priest welcomes us.

Penitential Rite

We remember our sins and ask God for mercy.

Gloria

We praise God in song.

Opening Prayer

We ask God to hear our prayers.

Liturgy of the Word
hearing God's plan of salvation

First Reading

We listen to God's Word, usually from the Old Testament.

Responsorial Psalm

We respond to God's Word in song.

Second Reading

We listen to God's Word from the New Testament.

Gospel Acclamation

We sing "Alleluia!" (except during Lent) to praise God for the Good News.

Gospel

We stand and listen to the Gospel of the Lord.

Homily

The priest or deacon explains God's Word.

Profession of Faith

We proclaim our faith through the Creed.

General Intercessions

We pray for our needs and the needs of others.

Liturgy of the Eucharist
celebrating Jesus' presence in the Eucharist

Preparation of the Altar and the Gifts

We bring gifts of bread and wine to the altar.

- Prayer Over the Gifts—The priest prays that God will accept our sacrifice.

Eucharistic Prayer

This prayer of thanksgiving is the center and high point of the entire celebration.

- Consecration—
  The bread and
  wine become the
  Body and Blood
  of Jesus Christ.

Communion Rite

We prepare to receive the Body and Blood
of Jesus Christ.

- Lord's Prayer—We pray the Our Father.
- Sign of Peace—We offer one another
  Christ's peace.
- Lamb of God—We pray for forgiveness, mercy,
  and peace.
- Communion—We receive the Body and Blood
  of Jesus Christ.

Concluding Rite
going forth to serve the Lord and others

Blessing

We receive God's blessing.

Dismissal

We go in peace to love and serve the
Lord and one another.

Receiving Communion

When we go to communion, we receive the Body of Christ—in the form of bread—in our hands or on our tongues. The priest or the eucharistic minister says, "The Body of Christ." We reply, "Amen."

We can also receive the Blood of Christ—in the form of wine. The priest or the minister offers the cup and says, "The Blood of Christ." We reply, "Amen." We take the cup in our hands and drink from it, and we then hand it back to the priest or eucharistic minister.

Holy Days of Obligation

Holy Days of Obligation are the days other than Sundays on which Catholics gather for Mass to celebrate the great things God has done for us through Jesus and the saints.

Six Holy Days of Obligation are celebrated in the United States.

January 1—Mary, Mother of God

40th day after Easter—Ascension

August 15—Assumption of the Blessed Virgin Mary

November 1—All Saints

December 8—Immaculate Conception

December 25—Nativity of Our Lord Jesus Christ

People and Things I See at Mass

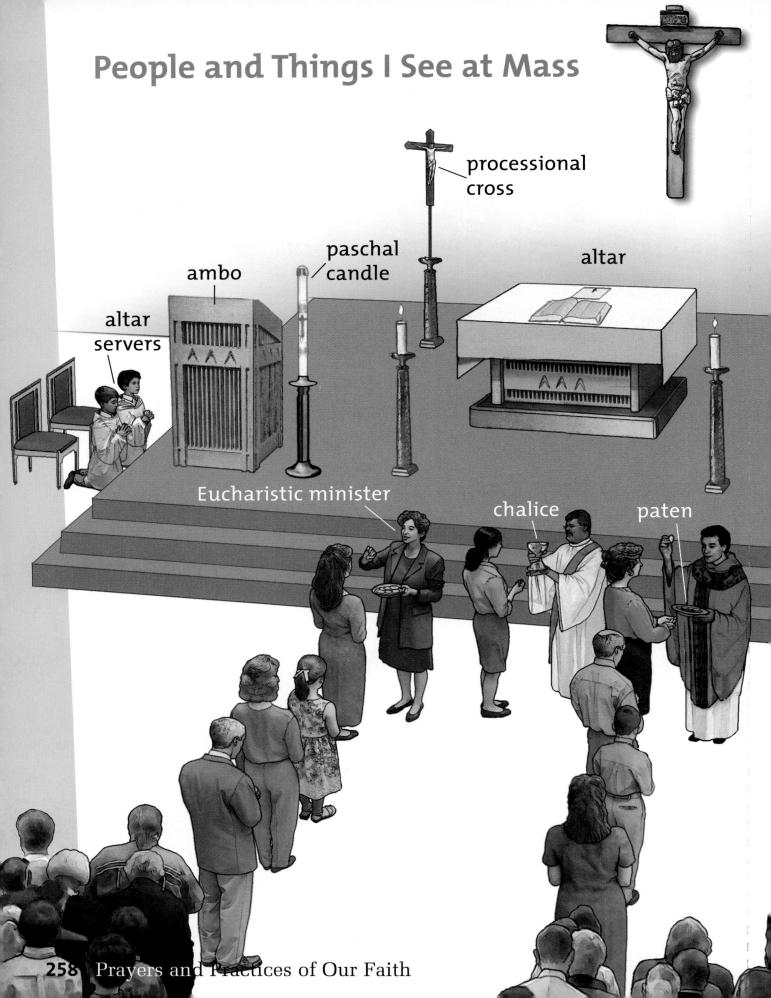

processional cross

paschal candle

ambo

altar

altar servers

Eucharistic minister

chalice

paten

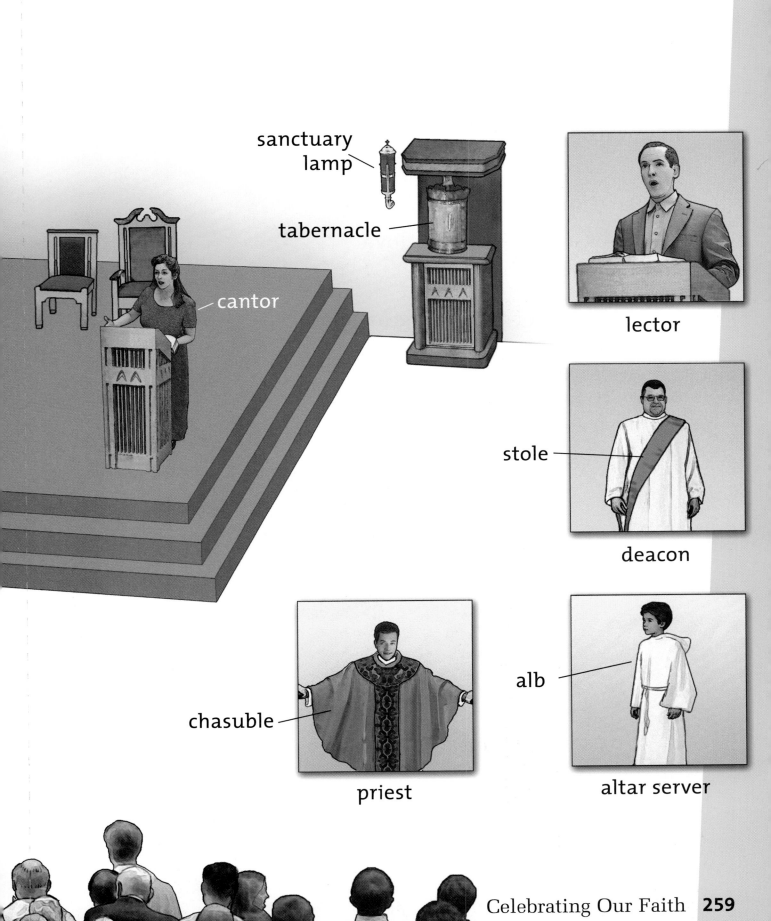

sanctuary lamp

tabernacle

cantor

lector

stole

deacon

chasuble

priest

alb

altar server

Celebrating Our Faith **259**

An Examination of Conscience

An examination of conscience is the act of reflecting on how we have hurt our relationships with God and others. Questions such as the following will help us in our examination of conscience:

My Relationship With God

Do I use God's name with love and reverence?

What steps am I taking to grow closer to God and to others?

Do I actively participate at Mass on Sundays and holy days?

Do I pray?

My Relationship With Family, Friends, and Neighbors

Have I set a bad example by my words or actions? Do I treat others fairly?

Am I loving to those in my family? Am I respectful of my neighbors, my friends, and those in authority?

Do I show respect for my body and for the bodies of others?

Have I taken or damaged anything that did not belong to me? Have I cheated or lied?

Do I quarrel or fight with others? Do I try to hurt people who I think have hurt me?

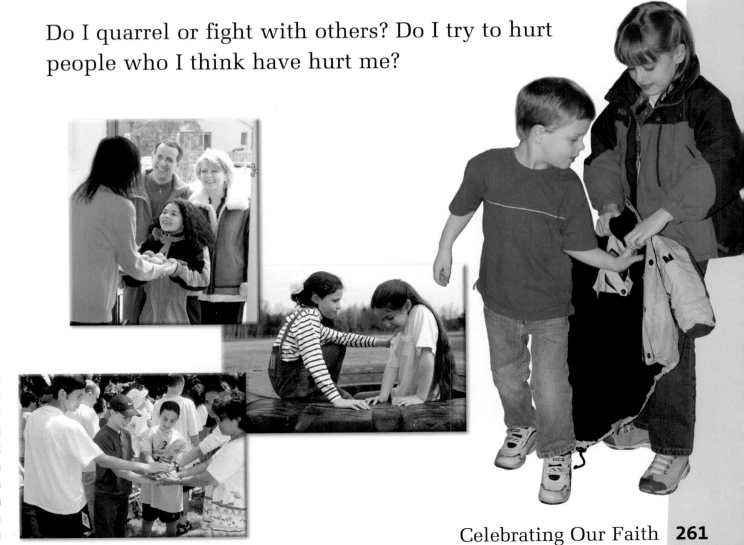

How to Go to Confession

An examination of conscience is an important part of preparing for the Sacrament of Penance. The Sacrament of Penance includes the following steps:

1. The priest greets us, and we pray the Sign of the Cross. He invites us to trust in God. He may read God's Word with us.

2. We confess our sins. The priest may help and counsel us.

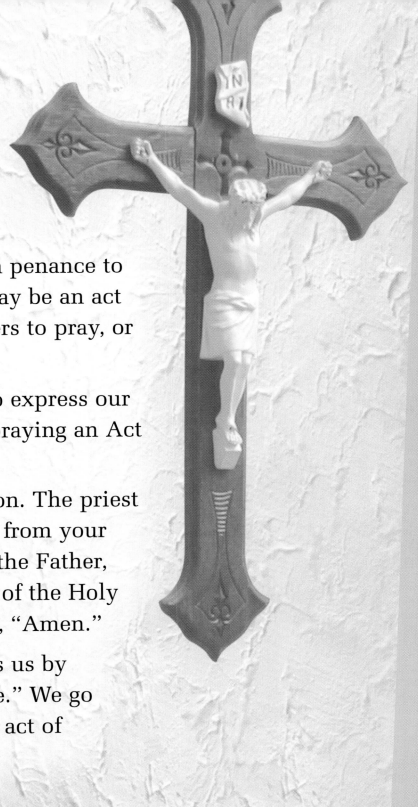

3. The priest gives us a penance to perform. Penance may be an act of kindness or prayers to pray, or both.

4. The priest asks us to express our sorrow, usually by praying an Act of Contrition.

5. We receive absolution. The priest says, "I absolve you from your sins in the name of the Father, and of the Son, and of the Holy Spirit." We respond, "Amen."

6. The priest dismisses us by saying, "Go in peace." We go forth to perform the act of penance he has given us.

The Ten Commandments

God gave us the Ten Commandments. They teach us how to live for God and for others. They help us follow the moral law to do good and avoid evil.

1. I am your God; love nothing more than me.

2. Use God's name with respect.

3. Keep the Lord's day holy.

4. Honor and obey your parents.

5. Treat all human life with respect.

6. Respect married life.

7. Respect what belongs to others.

8. Tell the truth.

9. Respect your neighbors and your friends.

10. Be happy with what you have.

The Great Commandment

People asked Jesus, "What is the most important commandment?" Jesus said, "First, love God. Love him with your heart, soul, and mind. The second is like it: Love your neighbor as much as you love yourself."

adapted from Matthew 22:37-39

We call this the Great Commandment.

The New Commandment

Before his death on the cross, Jesus gave his disciples a new commandment: "Love one another. As I have loved you, so you also should love one another."

John 13:34

The Beatitudes

Jesus gave us the Beatitudes in the Sermon on the Mount. They show us the way to true happiness.

Blessed are those who are kind to others.
They will be rewarded.

Blessed are those who do the right thing even when it is difficult.
They will be with God one day.

Blessed are those who are fair to others.
They will be treated fairly.

Blessed are those who work for peace.
They are God's children.

adapted from Matthew 5:1-10

Making Good Choices

The Holy Spirit helps us to make good choices. We get help from the Ten Commandments, the grace of the sacraments, and the teachings of the Church. We also get help from the example of the saints and fellow Christians. To make good choices, we ask the following questions:

1. Is the thing I am choosing to do a good thing?

2. Am I choosing to do it for the right reasons?

3. Am I choosing to do it at the right time and in the right place?

Fruits of the Holy Spirit

When we realize that the Holy Spirit lives within us, we live the way God wants us to. The Fruits of the Holy Spirit are signs of the Holy Spirit's action in our lives. They include the following:

love	generosity	peace
kindness	faithfulness	patience
gentleness	self-control	joy

Church Tradition also includes **goodness, modesty**, and **chastity** among the Fruits of the Holy Spirit.

Showing Our Love for the World

Jesus taught us to care for those in need. The social teachings of the Church call us to follow Jesus' example in each of the following areas:

Life and Dignity

God wants us to care for everyone. We are all made in his image.

Family and Community

Jesus wants us to be loving helpers in our families and communities.

Rights and Responsibilities

All people should have what they need to live good lives.

FREE HEALTH SCREENING

The Poor and Vulnerable

Jesus calls us to do what we can
to help people in need.

Work and Workers

The work that we do gives glory to God.

Solidarity

Since God is our Father, we are called to treat
everyone in the world as a brother or a sister.

God's Creation

We show our love for God's world by
taking care of it.

Food Drive

Song of Love

Chorus

Thank you Je - sus for help - ing me to

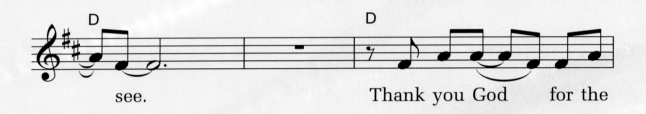

see. Thank you God for the

heart you've giv - en me.

Thank you Spir - it   for com-ing to   me,

and for show - ing   me how to   sing

your song of love.   (to Verse 1)

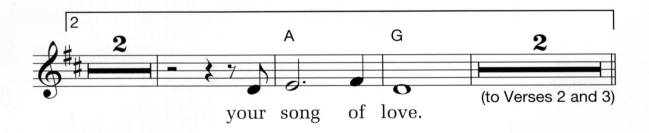

your song   of love.   (to Verses 2 and 3)

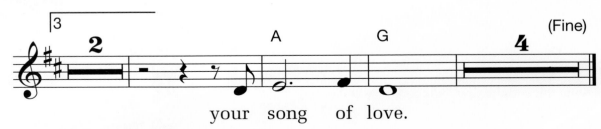

your song   of love.

continued

Song of Love *(continued)*

Verse 1

I saw some-one lone-ly by the road,

Some-one my age sad-ly all a - lone.

I shared my friend-ship and we talked a while.

(to Chorus)

I gave a hand, Je - sus gave back a smile.

"Echo" Holy, Holy

Ho - ly, Ho - ly, Ho - ly,

Lord, God of pow - er and might;

Heav - en, heav - en and earth

are full of your glo - ry.

Chorus

Sing Ho - san - na, (sing Ho - san - na,)

sing Ho - san - na, (sing Ho - san - na,)

sing Ho - san - na, (sing Ho - san - na,)

sing al - le - lu - ia.

(sing al - le - lu - ia.) (Fine)

Bless - ed, bless - ed is He,

(Bless - ed, bless - ed is He,) Who

comes in the Name of the Lord. (Who

comes in the Name of the Lord.) (to Chorus)

Songs of Our Faith **275**

Jesus in the Morning (Jesus verses)

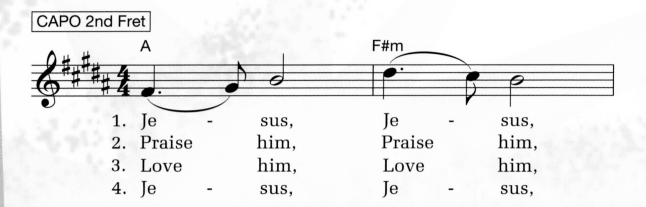

CAPO 2nd Fret

A   F#m

1. Je - sus,   Je - sus,
2. Praise   him,   Praise   him,
3. Love   him,   Love   him,
4. Je - sus,   Je - sus,

D   E

1. Je - sus in the morn-ing,   Je - sus in the noon-time;
2. Praise him in the morn-ing,   Praise him in the noon-time;
3. Love him in the morn-ing,   Love him in the noon-time;
4. Je - sus in the morn-ing,   Je - sus in the noon-time;

1. Je - sus, Je - sus,
2. Praise him, Praise him,
3. Love him, Love him,
4. Je - sus, Je - sus,

1. Je - sus when the sun goes down!
2. Praise him when the sun goes down!
3. Love him when the sun goes down!
4. Je - sus when the sun goes down!

"Jesus in the Morning" text and tune from traditional African-American folksong.

Songs of Our Faith **277**

Jesus in the Morning (Spirit verses)

CAPO 2nd Fret

1. Spir - it,   Spir - it,
2. Calls   me,   Calls   me,
3. Loves   me,   Loves   me,
4. Spir - it,   Spir - it,

1. Spir - it in the morn - ing, Spir - it in the noon - time;
2. Calls me in the morn - ing, Calls me in the noon - time;
3. Loves me in the morn - ing, Loves me in the noon - time;
4. Spir - it in the morn - ing, Spir - it in the noon - time;

1. Spir - it,   Spir - it,
2. Calls   me,   Calls   me,
3. Loves   me,   Loves   me,
4. Spir - it,   Spir - it,

1. Spir - it when the sun goes down!
2. Calls me when the sun goes down!
3. Loves me when the sun goes down!
4. Spir - it when the sun goes down!

"Jesus in the Morning" text and tune from traditional African-American folksong.

Songs of Our Faith **279**

Our Father

CAPO 1st Fret

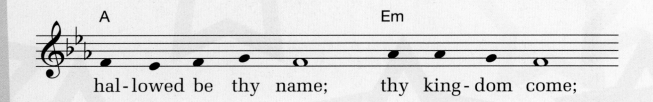

D

Our Fa - ther, who art in heav - en,

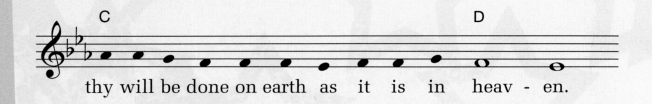

A   Em

hal - lowed be thy name;   thy king - dom come;

C   D

thy will be done on earth as it is in heav - en.

Em   C

Give us this day our dai - ly bread;

280 Prayers and Practices of Our Faith

and for - give us our tres - pass - es

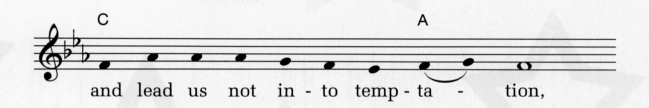

as we for - give those who tres - pass a - gainst us;

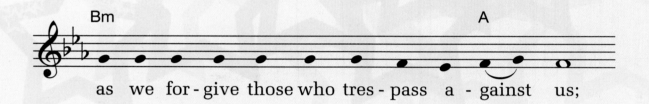

and lead us not in - to temp - ta - tion,

but de - liv - er us from e - vil. A - men.

"Our Father" tune from traditional chant.

Songs of Our Faith **281**

Friends, All Gather 'Round

Refrain (Repeat Refrain first time only.)

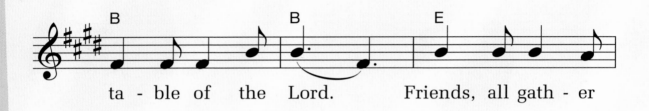

Friends, all gath - er 'round the

ta - ble of the Lord. Friends, all gath - er

'round the ta - ble of the Lord.

Verses

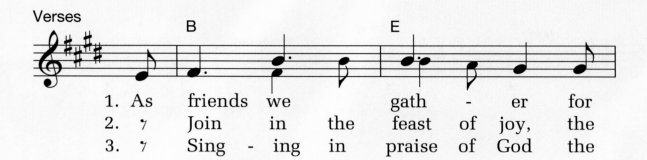

1. As friends we gath - er for
2. ⁊ Join in the feast of joy, the
3. ⁊ Sing - ing in praise of God the

1. friends we have be- come. Friends, all gath - er
2. ban - quet ta - ble of love. Friends, all gath - er
3. giv - er of good gifts. Friends, all gath - er

(to Refrain)

1. 'round the ta - ble of the Lord.
2. 'round the ta - ble of the Lord.
3. 'round the ta - ble of the Lord.

A Man Named Zacchaeus

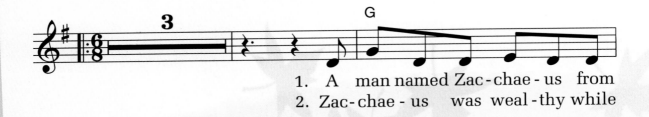

1. A man named Zac - chae - us from
2. Zac - chae - us was weal - thy while

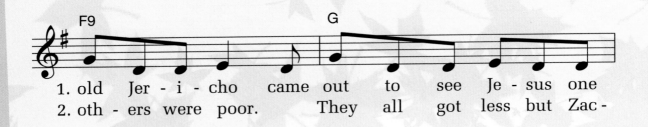

1. old Jer - i - cho came out to see Je - sus one
2. oth - ers were poor. They all got less but Zac -

1. day long a - go.
2. chae - us got more.

1. Zac - chae - us   was short, but he   want - ed   to   see.
2. ⁊ "Come down, Zac - chae - us," said   Je - sus, "Come down.

1. So   up,   up   he climbed in   a   syc - a - more tree.
2. ⁊   I'll   be   your friend, but you must turn a - round."

1. Zac - chae - us   was short, but he   want - ed   to   see.
2. ⁊ "Come down, Zac - chae - us," said   Je - sus, "Come down.

1. So   up,   up   he climbed in   a   syc - a - more tree.
2. ⁊   I'll   be   your friend, but you must turn a - round."

continued

A Man Named Zacchaeus *(continued)*

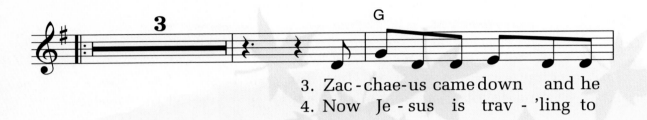

3. Zac-chae-us came down and he
4. Now Je - sus is trav - 'ling to

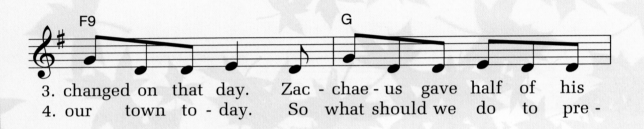

3. changed on that day. Zac - chae - us gave half of his
4. our town to - day. So what should we do to pre -

3. mon - ey a - way.
4. pare him a way?

3. Now he's the hap - pi - est per - son in town.
4. Feed all the hun - gry and care for the poor,

3. Zac - chae - us was lost, but now he is found.
4. then Je - sus will stay with us for - ev - er more.

3. Now he's the hap - pi - est per - son in town.
4. Feed all the hun - gry and care for the poor,

3. Zac - chae - us was lost, but now he is found.
4. then Je - sus will stay with us for - ev - er more.

Songs of Our Faith   **287**

Jesus, Jesus

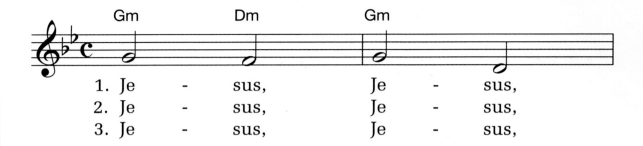

1. Je - sus, Je - sus,
2. Je - sus, Je - sus,
3. Je - sus, Je - sus,

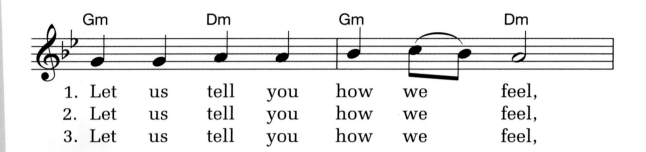

1. Let us tell you how we feel,
2. Let us tell you how we feel,
3. Let us tell you how we feel,

1. You have made Your home with - in us,
2. You have giv - en us Your for - give - ness,
3. You have giv - en us Your mer - cy,

1. we love you so.
2. we love you so.
3. we love you so.

(last time only)

You have giv - en us Your mer - cy,

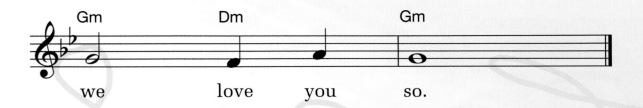

we love you so.

We Come to Your Table

Verses

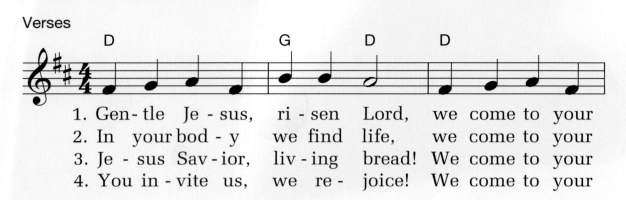

1. Gen-tle Je-sus, ri-sen Lord, we come to your
2. In your bod-y we find life, we come to your
3. Je-sus Sav-ior, liv-ing bread! We come to your
4. You in-vite us, we re-joice! We come to your

1. ta-ble; with our hearts so full of joy,
2. ta-ble; life you give for us to share,
3. ta-ble; Bread of heav-en, bread of hope.
4. ta-ble; We re-mem-ber, we give thanks!

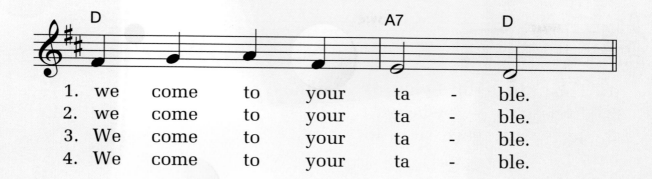

1. we come to your ta - ble.
2. we come to your ta - ble.
3. We come to your ta - ble.
4. We come to your ta - ble.

Refrain

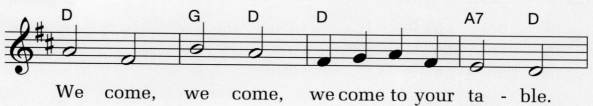

We come, we come, we come to your ta - ble.

We come, we come, we come to your ta - ble.

This Little Light of Mine

1. This lit - tle light of mine
2. Ev - 'ry - where I go,
3. Je - sus gave it to me,

1. I'm gon - na let it shine,
2. I'm gon - na let it shine,
3. I'm gon - na let it shine,

1. This lit - tle light of mine
2. Ev - 'ry - where I go,
3. Je - sus gave it to me,

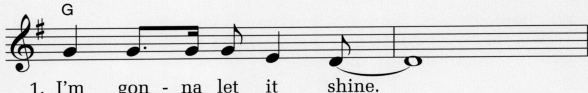

1. I'm gon - na let it shine.
2. I'm gon - na let it shine.
3. I'm gon - na let it shine.

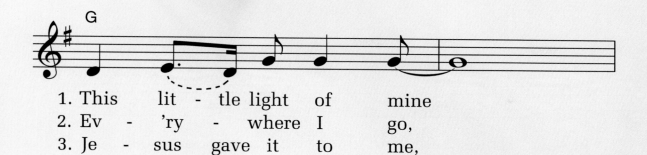

1. This lit - tle light of mine
2. Ev - 'ry - where I go,
3. Je - sus gave it to me,

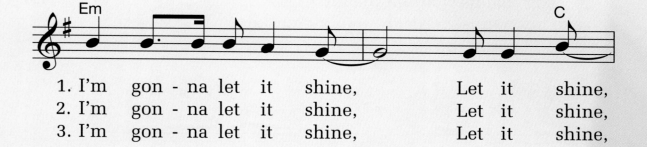

1. I'm gon - na let it shine, Let it shine,
2. I'm gon - na let it shine, Let it shine,
3. I'm gon - na let it shine, Let it shine,

1. _____ let it shine, let it shine.
2. _____ let it shine, let it shine.
3. _____ let it shine, let it shine.

"This Little Light of Mine" text and tune from traditional African-American spiritual.

Jesus' Hands Were Kind Hands

1. Je - sus' hands were kind hands, do - ing good to all,
2. Take my hands, Lord Je - sus, let them work for you;
3. Je - sus' hands were kind hands, do - ing good to all,
4. Take my hands, Lord Je - sus, let them work for you;

1. Heal - ing pain and sick - ness, bless-ing chil - dren small.
2. Make them strong and gen - tle, kind in all I do.
3. Heal - ing pain and sick - ness, bless-ing chil - dren small.
4. Make them strong and gen - tle, kind in all I do.

1. Wash-ing tir - ed feet, and sav - ing those who fall;
2. Let   me watch you, Je - sus, till I'm gen - tle too,
3. Wash-ing tir - ed feet, and sav - ing those who fall;
4. Let   me watch you, Je - sus, till I'm gen - tle too,

1. Je - sus' hands were kind hands, do - ing good to   all.
2. Till my hands are kind hands, quick to work for you.
3. Je - sus' hands were kind hands, do - ing good to   all.
4. Till my hands are kind hands, quick to work for you.

Glossary

A

absolution the forgiveness of God. In the Sacrament of Penance, we say that we are sorry for our sins. Then the priest offers us God's absolution. [absolución]

Advent the four weeks before Christmas. It is a time of joyful preparation for the celebration of Jesus' birth. [Adviento]

Advent wreath

All Saints Day November 1, the day on which the Church honors all who have died and now live with God as saints in heaven. These saints include all those who have been declared saints by the Church and many others known only to God. [Día de Todos los Santos]

All Souls Day November 2, the day on which the Church remembers all who have died as friends of God. We pray that they may rest in peace. [Día de Difuntos]

altar the table in the church on which the priest celebrates Mass. On this table, the bread and wine are offered to God to become the Body and Blood of Jesus Christ. [altar]

ambo a platform from which a person reads the Word of God during Mass [ambón]

altar

Amen the last word in any prayer that we pray. *Amen* means "This is true." We pray "Amen" to show that we really mean the words we have just said. [Amén]

angel a messenger from God [ángel]

Ash Wednesday the first day of Lent, on which we receive ashes on our foreheads to remind us to show sorrow for the choices we make that hurt our friendships with God and others [Miércoles de Ceniza]

B

Baptism the first of the three sacraments by which we become members of the Church. Baptism frees us from original sin and gives us new life in Jesus Christ through the Holy Spirit. [bautismo]

Beatitudes the eight ways we can behave in order to lead a Christian life. Jesus explains that if we live according to the Beatitudes, we are living as his followers. [Bienaventuranzas]

Bible the written story of God's promise to care for us, especially through his Son, Jesus [Biblia]

bishop a leader in the Church. Bishops teach us what God is asking of us as followers of Jesus today. [obispo]

Blessed Sacrament the bread that has been consecrated by the priest at Mass. It is kept in the tabernacle to adore and to be taken to the sick and the dying. [Santísimo Sacramento]

bishop

Body and Blood of Christ the bread and wine that has been consecrated by the priest at Mass [Cuerpo y Sangre de Cristo]

C

catholic a word that means "all over the world." The Church is catholic because Jesus gave the Church to the whole world. [católico]

Christ a title, like Messiah, that means "anointed with oil." This name is given to Jesus after the Resurrection. [Cristo]

Christian the name given to people who want to live as Jesus taught us to live [cristiano]

Christmas the day on which we celebrate the birth of Jesus [Navidad]

Church the name given to the followers of Christ all over the world. Spelled with a small *c*, church is the name of the building in which we gather to pray to God. [Iglesia]

Christmas caroling

commandment a rule that tells us how to live as God wants us to live [mandamiento]

confession the act of telling our sins to a priest in the Sacrament of Penance [confesión]

Confirmation the sacrament that completes the grace we receive in Baptism [confirmación]

conscience the inner voice that helps each of us to know what God wants us to do [conciencia]

Understanding the Words of Our Faith **299**

consecration the making of a thing or person to be special to God through prayer. At Mass the words of the priest are a consecration of the bread and wine. This makes them the Body and Blood of Jesus Christ. [consagración]

consecration

contrition the sadness we feel when we know that we have sinned [contrición]

creation everything that God has made. God said that all of creation is good. [creación]

Creator God, who made everything that is [Creador]

crozier the staff carried by a bishop. This staff shows that the bishop cares for us in the same way that a shepherd cares for his sheep. [báculo]

D

deacon a man who accepts God's call to serve the Church. Deacons help the bishop and priests in the work of the church. [diácono]

disciple a person who is a follower of Jesus and tries to live as he did [discípulo]

E

Easter the celebration of the bodily raising of Jesus Christ from the dead. Easter is the most important Christian feast. [Pascua]

Emmanuel a name that means "God with us." It is a name given to Jesus. [Emanuel]

Eucharist the sacrament in which we give thanks to God for giving us Jesus Christ. We receive Jesus Christ in the bread and wine that is blessed at Mass. [Eucaristía]

examination of conscience thinking about what we have said or done that may have hurt our friendship with God or others [examen de conciencia]

F

faith a gift of God. Faith helps us to believe in God and live as he wants us to live. [fe]

forgiveness the act of being kind to people who have hurt us but then have said that they are sorry. God always forgives us when we say that we are sorry. We forgive others the way God forgives us. [perdón]

Fruits of the Holy Spirit the ways in which we act because God is alive in us [frutos del Espíritu Santo]

G

genuflect to show respect in church by touching a knee to the ground, especially in front of the tabernacle [genuflexión, hacer la]

God the Father, Son, and Holy Spirit. God created us, saves us, and lives in us. [Dios]

godparent a witness to Baptism. A godparent helps the baptized person to live as a follower of Jesus. [padrino/madrina de bautismo]

genuflect

grace the gift of God given to us without our earning it. Sanctifying grace fills us with God's life and makes us his friends. [gracia]

Great Commandment Jesus' important teaching that we are to love both God and other people [El Mandamiento Mayor]

H

heaven the life with God that is full of happiness and never ends [cielo]

holy showing the kind of life we live when we cooperate with the grace of God [santa]

Holy Communion

Holy Communion the consecrated bread and wine that we receive at Mass that is blessed and becomes the Body and Blood of Jesus Christ [Sagrada Comunión]

Holy Days of Obligation those days other than Sundays on which we celebrate the great things God has done for us through Jesus Christ [días de precepto]

Holy Family the family made up of Jesus; his mother, Mary; and his foster father, Joseph [Sagrada Familia]

Holy Spirit the third person of the Trinity, who comes to us in Baptism and fills us with God's life [Espíritu Santo]

holy water the water that has been blessed. It is used to remind us of our Baptism. [agua bendita]

The Holy Family with Lamb

homily an explanation of God's word. A homily explains the words of God that we hear in the Bible readings at church. [homilía]

hope the trust that God will always be with us. We also trust that he will make us happy now and help us to live in a way that keeps us with him forever. [esperanza]

J

Jesus the Son of God, who was born of the Virgin Mary, died, was raised from the dead, and saves us so that we can live with God forever [Jesús]

Joseph the foster father of Jesus, who was engaged to Mary when the angel announced that Mary would have a child through the power of the Holy Spirit [José]

K

Kingdom of God God's rule over us. We experience the Kingdom of God in part now. We will experience it fully in heaven. [Reino de Dios]

L

Last Supper the last meal Jesus ate with his disciples on the night before he died. Every Mass is a remembrance of that last meal. [Última Cena]

Lectionary the book from which the stories from the Bible are read at Mass [Leccionario]

Lent six weeks during which we prepare to celebrate, with special prayers and actions, the rising of Jesus from the dead at Easter. Jesus rose from the dead to save us. [Cuaresma]

liturgy the public prayer of the Church that celebrates the wonderful things God has done for us in Jesus Christ [liturgia]

Lectionary

Liturgy of the Eucharist the second half of the Mass. In this part of the Mass, the bread and wine are blessed and become the Body and Blood of Jesus Christ. We receive the Body and Blood of Jesus Christ in Holy Communion. [Liturgia de la Eucaristía]

Liturgy of the Word the first half of the Mass. During this part of the Mass, we listen to God's Word from the Bible. [Liturgia de la Palabra]

M

Magnificat Mary's song of praise to God. She praises him for the great things he has done for her and planned for us through Jesus. [Magníficat]

Mary the mother of Jesus. She is called "full of grace" because God chose her to be Jesus' mother. [María]

Mass our most important means of praying to God. At Mass we listen to God's Word, the Bible. We receive Jesus Christ in the bread and wine that has been blessed. [Misa]

Messiah a title, like Christ, that means "anointed with oil." *Messiah* also means "Savior." [Mesías]

Mary, *The Virgin at Prayer*

ministry the service, or work, done for others. Ministry is done by bishops, priests, and deacons in the celebration of the sacraments. All those baptized are called to different kinds of ministry in the liturgy and in serving the needs of others. [ministerio]

moral choice a choice to do what is right. We make moral choices because they are what we believe God wants. [opción moral]

mortal sin a serious choice to turn away from God [pecado mortal]

N

New Testament the story of Jesus and the early Church [Nuevo Testamento]

O

Old Testament the story of God's plan for the salvation of all people [Antiguo Testamento]

original sin the result of the sin of Adam and Eve. They disobeyed God and chose to follow their own will rather than God's will. [pecado original]

P

parable one of the simple stories that Jesus told to show us what God wants for the world [parábola]

parish a community of believers in Jesus Christ who meet regularly to worship God together [parroquia]

penance the turning away from sin because we want to live as God wants us to live (*See* Sacrament of Penance.) [penitencia]

Pentecost the 50th day after Jesus was raised from the dead. On this day the Holy Spirit was sent from heaven, and the Church was born. [Pentecostés]

petition a request of God asking for what we need made with the knowledge that he created us and wants to give us what we need [petición]

pope the bishop of Rome, successor of Saint Peter, and leader of the Roman Catholic Church [Papa]

praise our telling of the happiness we feel simply because God is so good [alabanza]

prayer our talking to God and listening to him in our hearts [oración]

priest a man who accepts God's special call to serve the Church. Priests guide the Church and lead it in the celebration of the sacraments. [sacerdote]

R

reconciliation making friends again after a friendship has been broken by some action or lack of action. In the Sacrament of Penance, we are reconciled with God, the Church, and others. [reconciliación]

Resurrection the bodily raising of Jesus Christ from the dead on the third day after he died on the cross [Resurrección]

rite the special form followed in celebrating each sacrament [rito]

S

sacrament the way in which God enters our life. Through simple objects such as water, oil, and bread, Jesus continues to bless us. [sacramento]

Sacrament of Penance the sacrament in which we celebrate God's forgiveness of our sins when we say to the priest that we are sorry for them [sacramento de la penitencia]

Sacrament of Penance

Sacraments of Initiation the sacraments that make us members of God's Church. They are Baptism, Confirmation, and the Eucharist. [sacramentos de iniciación]

Sacrifice of the Mass the sacrifice of Jesus on the cross. We remember Jesus' sacrifice every time we celebrate Mass. [Sacrificio de la Misa]

saint a holy person who has died as a true friend of God and now lives with God forever [santo]

Savior Jesus, the Son of God, who became human to make us friends with God again. The name *Jesus* means "God saves." [Salvador]

sin a choice we make that hurts our friendships with God and with other people [pecado]

T

tabernacle the container in which the Blessed Sacrament is kept so that Holy Communion can be taken to the sick and the dying [sagrario]

tabernacle

temptation a thought or feeling that can lead us to disobey God. Temptation can come either from outside us or inside us. [tentación]

Ten Commandments the ten rules that God gave to Moses. The Ten Commandments sum up God's law and show us how to live as his children. [Diez Mandamientos]

trespasses acts that harm others [ofensas]

Trinity the mystery of one God, existing in three persons: the Father, the Son, and the Holy Spirit [Trinidad]

V

venial sin a choice we make that weakens our relationship with God or other people [pecado venial]

Glosario

A

absolución perdón de Dios. En el sacramento de la penitencia, después de que decimos que nos arrepentimos de nuestros pecados, el sacerdote nos ofrece la absolución de Dios. [absolution]

Adviento las cuatro semanas antes de la Navidad. Es una época de alegre preparación para la celebración del nacimiento de Jesús. [Advent]

agua bendita agua que ha sido bendecida. Se usa para recordarnos de nuestro bautismo. [holy water]

alabanza nuestra expresión de la alegría que sentimos sencillamente porque Dios es tan bueno [praise]

altar mesa en las iglesias en la que el sacerdote celebra la Misa. En esta mesa, se ofrece a Dios el pan y el vino para que se conviertan en el Cuerpo y Sangre de Jesucristo. [altar]

ambón plataforma desde donde una persona lee la Palabra de Dios durante la Misa [ambo]

Amén última palabra de todas las oraciones que rezamos. *Amén* quiere decir "es verdad". Rezamos *Amén* para mostrar que lo que acabamos de decir va en serio. [Amen]

ángel mensajero de Dios [angel]

Antiguo Testamento la historia del plan de Dios para la salvación de toda la gente [Old Testament]

B

báculo vara que lleva un obispo. Al llevar esta vara, un obispo muestra que cuida de nosotros de la misma forma en que un pastor cuida sus ovejas. [crozier]

bautismo el primero de los tres sacramentos mediante los cuales pasamos a ser miembros de la Iglesia. El bautismo nos libera del pecado original y nos da una vida nueva en Jesucristo por medio del Espíritu Santo. [Baptism]

Biblia historia escrita de la promesa que hizo Dios de cuidar de nosotros, especialmente a través de su Hijo, Jesús [Bible]

Bienaventuranzas ocho formas en que podemos comportarnos para poder llevar una vida cristiana. Jesús nos explica que, si vivimos según las Bienaventuranzas, vivimos como seguidores suyos. [Beatitudes]

C

católica quiere decir "mundial". La Iglesia es católica porque Jesús la ha dado al mundo entero. [catholic]

cielo vida con Dios que está llena de felicidad y que nunca termina [heaven]

conciencia nuestra voz interior que nos guía a cada uno a hacer lo que Dios nos pide [conscience]

confesión acto de contar nuestros pecados al sacerdote en el sacramento de la penitencia [confession]

confirmación sacramento que completa la gracia que recibimos en el bautismo [Confirmation]

consagración el hacer a una cosa o persona especial ante los ojos de Dios por medio de la oración. En la Misa, las palabras del sacerdote son una consagración del pan y el vino. Esto los convierte en el Cuerpo y Sangre de Jesucristo. [consecration]

contrición tristeza que sentimos cuando sabemos que hemos pecado [contrition]

creación todo lo que hizo Dios. Dios dijo que toda de la creación es buena. [creation]

Creador Dios, quien hizo todo lo que es [Creator]

cristiano nombre dado a todos los que quieren vivir como Jesús nos enseñó [Christian]

Cristo que quiere decir "ungido". A Jesús se le título igual que Mesías llama así después de la Resurrección. [Christ]

Cuaresma las seis semanas en las que nos preparamos, con oraciones y acciones especiales, a celebrar en la Pascua la Resurrección de Jesús de entre los muertos. Jesús resucitó para salvarnos. [Lent]

Cuerpo y Sangre de Cristo pan y vino que han sido consagrados por el sacerdote en la Misa [Body and Blood of Christ]

D

Día de Difuntos el 2 de noviembre, día en que la Iglesia recuerda a todos los que han muerto como amigos de Dios. Nosotros rezamos por ellos para que descansen en paz. [All Souls Day]

Día de Todos los Santos el 1 de noviembre, día en que la Iglesia recuerda a todos los muertos que pasaron a ser santos y ahora viven con Dios en el cielo. Éstos son todos los muertos que han sido declarados santos por la Iglesia y otros que sólo Dios conoce. [All Saints Day]

diácono varón que acepta la llamada de Dios a servir la Iglesia. Los diáconos ayudan al obispo y a los sacerdotes en el trabajo de la Iglesia. [deacon]

días de precepto aquellos días que no sean domingos en que celebramos las grandes cosas que Dios ha hecho por nosotros a través de Jesucristo [Holy Days of Obligation]

Diez Mandamientos diez reglas que Dios dio a Moisés que resumen la ley de Dios y nos muestran cómo vivir como hijos suyos [Ten Commandments]

Dios Padre, Hijo, y Espíritu Santo. Dios nos creó, Él nos salva, y vive en nosotros. [God]

discípulo persona que sigue a Jesús y trata de vivir de la misma forma en que Él vivió [disciple]

E

Emanuel nombre que significa "Dios con nosotros". Es el nombre que se le da a Jesús. [Emmanuel]

esperanza confianza de que Dios estará siempre con nosotros. También confiamos en que Él nos dará felicidad ahora y nos ayudará a vivir de una forma que nos mantendrá con Él para siempre. [hope]

Espíritu Santo tercera persona de la Trinidad, que viene a nosotros en el bautismo y nos llena de la vida de Dios [Holy Spirit]

Eucaristía sacramento en el cual damos gracias a Dios por habernos dado a Jesucristo. Recibimos a Jesucristo en el pan y el vino que son consagrados en la Misa. [Eucharist]

examen de conciencia el pensar sobre lo que hemos dicho o hecho que pudo haber dañado nuestra amistad con Dios y con otras personas [examination of conscience]

F

fe don de Dios. La fe nos permite creer en Dios y vivir de la forma en que Él quiere que vivamos. [faith]

frutos del Espíritu Santo forma en que actuamos porque Dios vive en nosotros [Fruits of the Holy Spirit]

G

genuflexión, hacer la forma de mostrar respeto en la iglesia doblando una rodilla y haciéndola tocar el suelo, sobre todo cuando estamos delante del sagrario [genuflect]

gracia don de Dios que se nos da gratuitamente. La gracia sanctificante nos llena de la vida de Dios y nos hace sus amigos. [grace]

H

homilía explicación de la Palabra de Dios. Una homilía explica las palabras de Dios que oímos durante las lecturas de la Biblia en la iglesia. [homily]

I

Iglesia nombre que se le da a los seguidores de Jesús por todo el mundo. Si se escribe con "i" minúscula, quiere decir el edificio donde nos reunimos para orar a Dios. [Church]

J

Jesús Hijo de Dios, que nació de la Virgen María, murió, fue resucitado de entre los muertos, y nos salva para que pudiésemos vivir con Dios para siempre [Jesus]

José padre adoptivo de Jesús, que estaba desposado con María cuando el ángel anunció que ella tendría un hijo por obra del poder del Espíritu Santo [Joseph]

L

Leccionario libro del cual se leen en la Misa los relatos de la Biblia [Lectionary]

liturgia oración pública de la Iglesia que celebra las maravillas que Dios ha hecho por nosotros en Jesucristo [liturgy]

Liturgia de la Eucaristía la segunda de las dos partes de la Misa. En esta parte, se bendice el pan y el vino, que se convierten en el Cuerpo y Sangre de Jesucristo. Luego, recibimos el Cuerpo y Sangre de Cristo en la Sagrada Comunión. [Liturgy of the Eucharist]

Liturgia de la Palabra la primera de las dos partes de la Misa. Durante esta parte, oímos la Palabra de Dios en la Biblia. [Liturgy of the Word]

M

Magníficat canto de María de alabanza a Dios. Ella lo alaba por las grandes cosas que ha hecho por ella y los grandes planes que ha hecho para nosotros a través de Jesús. [Magnificat]

mandamiento regla que nos muestra cómo vivir de la forma en que Dios quiere que vivamos [commandment]

El Mandamiento Mayor enseñanza importante de Jesús de amar a Dios y a los demás [Great Commandment]

María madre de Jesús. Se le dice "llena de gracia" porque Dios la eligió para ser madre de Jesús. [Mary]

Mesías título igual que Cristo que quiere decir "ungido". Mesías significa también "Salvador". [Messiah]

Miércoles de Ceniza primer día de Cuaresma, en el que se nos coloca ceniza en la frente para que nos acordemos de mostrar arrepentimiento por decisiones que hemos tomado que dañan nuestra amistad con Dios y los demás [Ash Wednesday]

ministerio servicio, u obra, que se hace para otros. Lo hacen los obispos, sacerdotes, y diáconos en la celebración de los sacramentos. Todos los bautizados son llamados a distintos tipos de ministerio en la liturgia y en el servicio a las necesidades de los demás. [ministry]

Misa la forma más importante de rezar a Dios. En la Misa, oímos la Palabra de Dios en la Biblia y recibimos a Jesucristo en el pan y el vino bendecidos. [Mass]

N

Navidad día en que se festeja el nacimiento de Jesús [Christmas]

Nuevo Testamento la historia de Jesús y la Iglesia antigua [New Testament]

O

obispo uno de los líderes de la Iglesia. Los obispos nos enseñan lo que Dios nos pide hoy como seguidores de Jesús. [bishop]

ofensas daño que hacemos a otros [trespasses]

opción moral el elegir hacer lo que está bien. Elegimos opciones morales porque son lo que creemos que Dios quiere. [moral choice]

oración el hablar con Dios y escucharlo en nuestro corazón [prayer]

P

padrino/madrina de bautismo testigo de bautismo. El padrino o la madrina ayuda al bautizado a vivir como seguidor de Jesús. [godparent]

Papa el obispo de Roma, sucesor de San Pedro, y cabeza de la Iglesia católica romana [pope]

parábola una de las sencillas narraciones que Jesús contaba que nos muestran lo que Dios quiere para el mundo [parable]

parroquia comunidad de creyentes en Jesucristo que se reúne regularmente a orar a Dios [parish]

Pascua celebración de la resurrección corporal de Jesucristo de entre los muertos. La Pascua es la fiesta cristiana más importante. [Easter]

pecado decisión que daña nuestra amistad con Dios y con los demás [sin]

pecado mortal decisión grave que nos aparta de Dios [mortal sin]

pecado original resultado del pecado de Adán y Eva. Ellos desobedecieron a Dios y decidieron seguir su propia voluntad y no la de Dios. [original sin]

pecado venial decisión que debilita nuestra relación con Dios y los demás [venial sin]

penitencia el apartarnos del pecado porque queremos vivir de la forma en que Dios quiere que vivamos (*Véase* sacramento de la penitencia.) [penance]

Pentecostés el 50º día después de la resurrección de Jesús. En este día, el Espíritu Santo fue enviado del cielo y nació la Iglesia. [Pentecost]

perdón acto de ser buenos con personas que nos han hecho daño pero que después nos dicen que están arrepentidas. Dios siempre nos perdona cuando decimos que estamos arrepentidos. Nosotros perdonamos a los demás al igual que Dios nos perdona. [forgiveness]

petición el pedir a Dios lo que necesitamos porque Él nos ha creado y quiere darnos lo que necesitamos [petition]

R

reconciliación volver a ser amigos después de haberse roto una amistad por alguna acción o falta de acción. En el sacramento de la penitencia, nos reconciliamos con Dios, la Iglesia, y los demás. [reconciliation]

Reino de Dios dominio de Dios sobre nosotros. Experimentamos hoy el Reino de Dios en parte, pero lo experimentaremos por completo en el cielo. [Kingdom of God]

Resurrección el regreso a la vida del cuerpo de Jesucristo al tercer día después de haber muerto en la cruz [Resurrection]

rito cosas especiales que hacemos para celebrar cada sacramento [rite]

S

sacerdote varón que ha aceptado un llamado especial para servir a la Iglesia. Los sacerdotes guían a la Iglesia y presiden en la celebración de los sacramentos. [priest]

sacramento forma en que Dios entra en nuestra vida. Por medio de objetos sencillos, como el agua, el aceite, y el pan, Jesús sigue bendiciéndonos. [sacrament]

sacramento de la penitencia sacramento en el cual celebramos el perdón de Dios a nuestros pecados cuando decimos a un sacerdote que nos arrepentimos de ellos [Sacrament of Penance]

sacramentos de iniciación sacramentos que nos hacen miembros de la Iglesia de Dios. Son tres: bautismo, confirmación, y Eucaristía. [Sacraments of Initiation]

Sacrificio de la Misa sacrificio de Jesús en la cruz. Lo recordamos cada vez que celebramos la Misa. [Sacrifice of the Mass]

Sagrada Comunión pan y vino consagrados que recibimos en la Misa, los cuales son bendecidos y se convierten en el Cuerpo y Sangre de Jesucristo [Holy Communion]

Sagrada Familia familia compuesta por Jesús, su madre María, y su padre adoptivo José [Holy Family]

sagrario pieza donde se guarda el Santísimo Sacramento para que la Sagrada Comunión pueda ser llevada a los enfermos y a los moribundos [tabernacle]

Salvador Jesús, el Hijo de Dios, que se hizo hombre para que volvamos a ser amigos con Dios. El nombre *Jesús* quiere decir "Dios salva". [Savior]

santa tipo de vida que vivimos cuando cooperamos con la gracia de Dios [holy]

Santísimo Sacramento pan que ha sido consagrado por el sacerdote en la Misa. Se guarda en el sagrario para su adoración y para ser llevado a los enfermos y a los moribundos. [Blessed Sacrament]

santo persona virtuosa y ejemplar que ha muerto estando en amistad con Dios y que ahora vive con Él para siempre [saint]

T

tentación pensamiento o sentimiento que puede llevar a desobedecer a Dios. La tentación puede venir de fuera o de dentro de nosotros mismos. [temptation]

Trinidad misterio de la existencia de un Dios en tres personas: Padre, Hijo, y Espíritu Santo [Trinity]

U

Última Cena última comida que cenaron Jesús y sus discípulos en la noche antes de que muriera. Cada Misa es un recordatorio de esa última cena. [Last Supper]

Acknowledgments

Excerpts from the English translation of *Rite of Baptism for Children* © 1969, International Commission on English in the Liturgy, Inc. (ICEL); excerpts from the English translation of *The Roman Missal* © 1973, ICEL; excerpts from the English translation of *A Book of Prayers* © 1982, ICEL; excerpts from the English translation of *Book of Blessings* © 1988, ICEL. All rights reserved. Used with permission.

Excerpts from *The New American Bible with Revised New Testament and Psalms* Copyright © 1991, 1986, 1970 Confraternity of Christian Doctrine, Inc., Washington, DC. Used with permission. All rights reserved. No portion of the *New American Bible* may be reprinted without permission in writing from the copyright holder.

Illustration

Peter Church: 12, 13, 14, 28, 29, 42, 44, 45, 46, 52, 54, 60, 61, 68, 69, 92, 93, 100, 101, 108, 109, 124, 132, 148, 164–165, 173, 180–181, 188, 207, 208, 211, 215, 216, 223, 224

Doron Ben Ami: 249, 258–259, 268–269

Julie Downing: 53, 55, 85, 107, 117, 123, 125, 133, 152, 173, 175, 198, 205, 210, 214, 220, 232, 233, 246, 251, 252, 255, 267

Jim Effler: 4, 5, 7, 20, 21, 35, 246–247, 248–249

Tom Foty: 11, 47, 48, 65, 96, 99, 112, 118, 131, 135, 136, 139, 140, 141, 142, 150, 155, 158–159, 166, 167, 174, 190, 195, 204, 213, 225, 226, 227, 237, 243, 250, 251, 252, 253, 254

Ed Gazsi: 1, 2, 41, 42, 62, 81, 82, 121, 122, 161, 162, 183, 188, 191

Fran Gregory: 242, 243

Vitali Konstantinov: 201

David LaFleur: 240, 241

John Stevens: 38, 250, 251, 252, 253, 254, 255, 266

Susan Tolonen: 238, 239

Olwyn Whelan: 37, 59, 62, 71, 76, 111, 157, 205, 217, 238

Photography

Unless otherwise acknowledged, photographs are the property of Loyola Press. Page positions are abbreviated as follows: (t) top, (m) middle, (b) bottom, (l) left, (r) right, (l-r) left to right, (bkgr) background, (ins) inset, (cl) clockwise from top right, (all) all images on page.

UNIT 1: 2 (bkgr) © Georg Gerster/Photo Researchers. **3** (cl) photodisc/Getty Images; © Russell Kaye/Getty Images; © Phil Martin Photography; photodisc/Getty Images; © Royalty-Free/CORBIS. **6** © Stephen Simpson/Getty Images; (ins) photodisc/Getty Images. **8** Courtesy of Subaru Telescope, National Astronomical Observatory of Japan. **9** © Peter Corez/Getty Images; (ins) photodisc/Getty Images. **10** (b,l) photodisc/Getty Images; (t,r) © The Crosiers/Gene Plaisted OSC; (m,r) © Jeff Greenberg/Index Stock; (b,r) © Myrleen F. Cate/PhotoEdit; (b,r) photodisc/Getty Images. **15** © Phil Martin Photography. **16** © Rick Etkin/Getty Images. **17** © Phil Martin Photography. **18** (t,l) Fr. William Hart McNichols; (m,l) © Tony Freeman/PhotoEdit; (b,l) Courtesy Hugo Gutierrez Cordero, Peru; (r) photodisc/Getty Images. **19** © Jose Carillo/PhotoEdit. **22** (l) © Myrleen F. Cate/Index Stock Imagery/PictureQuest; (r) © Peter Cade/Getty Images; (bkgr) Peter Miller/Panoramic Images. **23** (bkgr) Peter Miller/Panoramic Images; (ins) © Phil Deggenger. **24** Jesse Ceballos/SuperStock. **26** (t,l) © Norbert Schaefer/CORBIS; (b,l) © Raoul Minsart/CORBIS; (r) © Myrleen F. Cate/PhotoEdit. **27** (l) © Phil Martin Photography; (m) © Arthur Tilley/Getty Images; (r) © Phil Martin Photography. **30** (cl) © AJA Productions/Getty Images; © Phil Martin Photography; © Laura Dwight/PhotoEdit; (bkgr) photodisc/Getty Images. **31** (cl) © Owen Franken/Getty Images; © Mark Segal/Getty Images; © Walter Hodges/Getty Images; (bkgr) photodisc/Getty Images. **32** © Phil Martin Photography. **33** © Robert E. Daemmrich/Getty Images; (leaves) photodisc/Getty Images. **34** (t,l) © Cameraphoto/Art Resource, NY; (b,l) © The Crosiers/Gene Plaisted OSC; (r) photodisc/Getty Images. **35** (ins,t) photodisc/Getty Images; (ins,b) © Myrleen F. Cate/PhotoEdit. **36** Woo Ching Man, 11, Hong Kong. From the worldwide competition: "Children of the World Illustrate the Bible" by MallMedia publishing house, www.bible2000.com. **39** © Phil Martin Photography. **40** © Phil Martin Photography.

UNIT 2: 43 (t,l) © Jeff Greenberg/PhotoEdit; (b,l) © David Young-Wolff/PhotoEdit; (r) © Cameron/CORBIS. **49** Inc. G&J Images/Getty Images. **50** (l) © Don Hammond/CORBIS; (t,r) © Hoa Qui/Index Stock Imagery/PictureQuest. **51** (cl) © Ross Whitaker; © Michael Newman/PhotoEdit; photodisc/Getty Images. **55** Dennis DeBasco, Abbot, Inclusive Orthodox Church. **56** © Myrleen F. Cate/PhotoEdit. **57** (t) © Robert Brenner/PhotoEdit; (m) photodisc/Getty Images. **58** (t,l) © Tate Gallery, London/Art Resource, NY; (m) photodisc/Getty Images; (b,r) photodisc/Getty Images. **59** (l) photodisc/Getty Images; (tr) © Arthur Tilley/Getty Images. **63** (l) Vittoriano Rastelli/CORBIS; (t,r) © Bettmann/CORBIS; (b,r) SIPA Press. **64** © Annie Griffiths Belt/CORBIS. **66** (l) © Jose Luis Pelaez, Inc./CORBIS; (t,r) © AFP/CORBIS; (m,r) photodisc/Getty Images; (b,r) Richard Hutchings/PhotoEdit. **70** © John H. White. **72** © Phil Martin Photography. **73** (t) © Michelle D. Bridwell/PhotoEdit; (m) photodisc/Getty Images. **74** (l) photodisc/Getty Images; (t,r) Elizabeth Lee Hudgins/iconsof thefaith.com; (b,r) photodisc/Getty Images. **75** (l) © Steve Niedorf/Getty Images; (r) © Yellow Dog Productions/Getty Images. **77** (t,l) © Royalty-free/CORBIS; (b,l) © Phil Martin Photography; (r) © Royality-free/CORBIS. **79** © The Crosiers/Gene Plaisted OSC. **80** © The Crosiers/Gene Plaisted OSC.

UNIT 3: 82 (bkgr) © John Quinn SJ. **83** (l) © Myrleen F. Cate/PhotoEdit; (m) © Richard Hutchings/CORBIS; (t,r) © Myrleen F. Cate/PhotoEdit. **84** (l) © Richard Hutchings/PhotoEdit; (t,r) © Phil Martin Photography. **86** (cl) © Myrleen F. Cate/PhotoEdit; photodisc/Getty Images; photodisc/Getty Images; © Myrleen F. Cate/PhotoEdit. **87** © Stephen McBrady/PhotoEdit. **88** © Robert Houser/Index Stock Imagery/PictureQuest. **90** (l) Courtesy of The Christophers; (t,r) © The Crosiers/Gene Plaisted OSC; (m,r) photodisc/Getty Images; (b,r) photodisc/Getty Images. **109** (b,r) photodisc/Getty Images. **98** (t,l) © Hurewitz Creative/CORBIS; (m,l) © Jeff Greenberg/PhotoEdit; (b,l) © Jim Whitmer Photography. **104** © Anthony Moreland/Getty Images. **105** © Jonathan Nourok/PhotoEdit. **106** (t,l) © James Frank/Stock Connection/PictureQuest; (b,l) © Joel Sartore/CORBIS; (t,r) Courtesy of National Library of Greece; (b,r) © Peter Hince/Getty Images. **107** (cl) © Myrleen F. Cate/PhotoEdit; photodisc/Getty Images; photodisc/Getty Images. **111** © The Crosiers/Gene Plaisted OSC. **114** (t,l) © Scala/Art Resource, NY; (b,l) © Myrleen F. Cate/PhotoEdit; (r) photodisc/Getty Images. **115** (l) photodisc/Getty Images; (r) © FPG International/Getty Images. **119** © Phil Martin Photography. **120** © David Young-Wolff/PhotoEdit.

UNIT 4: 122 (bkgr) © Dennis Degnan/CORBIS. **123** (l) © Bonnie Kamin/PhotoEdit; (r) © Julie Habel/CORBIS. **125** (b,r) © Maureen Collins Photography. **126** (m) © Phil Martin Photography. **127** photodisc/Getty Images. **128** © Stephen Frink/CORBIS. **129** © Omni Photo Communications Inc./Index Stock. **130** (t,l) © Tony Hamblin/CORBIS; (m,l) © Stephen Derr/Getty Images; (b,l) © The Crosiers/Gene Plaisted OSC; (r) photodisc/Getty Images. **134** (l) © The Crosiers/Gene Plaisted OSC. **138** (l) © Regine M./Getty Images; (t,r) Vatican Museum of Modern Art; (m,r) © The Crosiers/Gene Plaisted OSC; (b,r) photodisc/Getty Images. **143** (bkgr) photodisc/Getty Images. **144** © Jim Whitmer Photography. **145** © Phyllis Picardi/Index Stock Imagery/PictureQuest. **146** (t,l) © The Crosiers/Gene Plaisted OSC; (b,l) © Jeff Greenberg/PhotoEdit; (t,r) © Mark E. Gibson/CORBIS; (b,r) © SW Production/Index Stock. **147** (l) © John Terence Turner/Getty Images; (t,r) © Earl Kowall/CORBIS. **151** (t,l) © Chip Henderson/Index Stock Imagery/PictureQuest; (b,l) photodisc/Getty Images; (t,r) photodisc/Getty Images; (b,r) © Myrleen F. Cate/PhotoEdit. **153** (t,r) © Brett Froomer; (m,r) photodisc/Getty Images. **154** (t,l) Cameramann, Int'l/Milton & Joan Mann; (b,l) V.C.L./Paul Viant/Getty Images; (t,r) © The Crosiers/Gene Plaisted OSC; (b,r) © The Crosiers/Gene Plaisted OSC. **160** (r) © Tony Freeman/PhotoEdit; (m) photodisc/Getty Images.

UNIT 5: 162 (bkgr) © Vanni Archive/CORBIS. **163** (l) © Myrleen F. Cate/PhotoEdit; (r) © Richard Hutchings/PhotoEdit. **168** photodisc/Getty Images. **170** (t,l) Coll. Kroller-Muller Museum, Otterlo; (b,l) © Joe McBride/CORBIS; (t,r) © Steve Chenn/CORBIS; (b,r) photodisc/Getty Images. **173** © Phil Martin Photography. **177** Courtesy Dahri Nelson/Trinity Lutheran School, Waconia, MN. **178** (t,l) © Scala, Art Resource, NY; (m,l) © The Crosiers/Gene Plaisted OSC; (b,l) photodisc/Getty Images;